HOW MANAGING ORGANIZATIONAL TIME

JOHN LOK

Contents

Preface   *v*

Prologue   *vii*

Time Pressure Influences Consumer Behavior

1. Consumer Behavioral Factors Influence Theory   3

2. How The Time Consumption Pressure Factor Influences   11
Irrational Consumption Decision Making

3. Reducing Time Pressure Consumption Methods   19

4. What Consumption Is Most Influenced In Preference Choice By   29
Time Pressure

5. May Time Dominate Consumption Final Purchase Decision   45
Making

6. Time Press How Influences Video Playing Game Consumer   56
Purchase Behavior

TIME PRESSURE INFLUENCE ENTREPRENEUR SUCCESS

7. Entrepreneurship Successful Factors   69

8. Time Queue Pressure Brings Theme Park Entertainment Industry   80
Visitors Negative Emotion

Consumer Psychology Time

9. Ready-food Meal Short Time Cooking Attractive Factor   103

10. Time Pressure Influences Traveller Behavior   112

Preface

Introduction

In this book, I explain why and how time factor will bring some product or service to let customers feel time pressure negative emotion or positive emotion. In chapter one, I shall explain how and why Walt Disney theme entertainment park which need to concern long time queue will bring negative emotion to its visitors and how it attempt to solve this long time queue challenge to change their emotion as well as how and why it can apply short time space tourism entertainment facility to let visitors to feel that they can spend short time to catch rocket to go to space tourism. In chapter two, I shall indicate why and how short time cooking factor will be any taste of read cooking meals' main attractive factor to influence food consumers prefer to choose to buy them to replace the fresh uncooked food in supermarkets or food stores. In chapter three, I shall explain how any why long time pressure will influence how to change travellers' shopping behaviors.

I shall explain how and why time pressure will influence marketing behavior. I shall indicate some service and product case to explain what the time pressure consumption environment can influence consumer decision making. I also indicate some large international organizations to explain how and why consumers will feel time pressure to influence their consumption behaviors. This second part explains how and why time pressure will influence employees feel that they need learn how to change their working behavior in order to adapt their working pressure environment.

In this book, however, I aim to research whether time factor can influence the consumer individual consumption desire to be changed either to choose to buy this product or consume this service or choose to buy another product or consume another service to replace the consumer whose original preference choice. If time factor can influence any one consumer individual consumption choice to be changed easily.

I shall indicate how time pressure can bring positive economy and psychology factors to influence enterprise success. I suppose any entrepreneur individual behavior will be influenced to decide to choose the best way to achieve whose strategy from both individual psychological factor influences and external economy environment factor influences by time pressure positive influence. I shall indicate how and why long time entertainment queue will bring pressure to influence theme park entertainment visitors to feel negative emotion.

It is suitable to any readers who have interesting to judge whether what economy and psychology factors will influence any enterprise success as well as how the entrepreneur can be influenced to do any right judgement to any entrepreneurial activities from economic environment factors and the entrepreneur individual psychological factors influence more easily.

Prologue

Table of content
    part 1
    Time pressure influences
consumer behavior
    Chapter 1
Consumer behavioral factors
influence theory p.4-16
    ● How and why time limiting pressure
influences consumer choice p.17-30
    Chapter 2
How the time consumption pressure
factor influences irrational
consumption decision making p.31-44
    ● Time pressure consumption decision
making process characteristics p.45-58
    Chapter 3
Reducing time pressure consumption
methods p.59-72
    ● What are the in-store and out-store
factors influence supermarket
fast moving consumer decision p.73-86
    Chapter 4
What consumption is most
influenced in preference choice
by time pressure p.87-100
    ● Time pressure impacts consumer
behavioral effect p.101-114
    ● The reasons cause consumers
feel time pressure p.115-128
    Chapter 5
May time dominate consumption
final purchase decision making p.129-144
    ● Methods avoid consumers
feel time pressure p.145-160

Chapter 6
Time press how influences
video playing game consumer
purchase behavior p.161-175
● Long time pressure brings
poor performance and customer
negative emotion reason p.176-190
part 2
TIME PRESSURE
INFLUENCE ENTREPRENEUR
SUCCESS

Chapter 7
Entrepreneurship successful factors
Entrepreneurial intentions p.191-124
Social capital
Attitude
Positive psychological factors
● Motivation factors influence entrepreneurs
on business surviving p.125-138
● Entrepreneurship innovation and economy growth influence to
entrepreneurs
Concept innovation factor p.139-152
How to avoid uncertain and risky outcomes
Reference
Chapter 8
Time queue pressure brings theme park entertainment
industry visitors negative emotion p.153-167
Reference

Part 3
Consumer psychological time

Chapter 9
Ready-food meal short
time cooking attractive factor p.168-183
Chapter 10
Time pressure influence s

traveller behavior p.184-203
    reference

Time pressure influences consumer behavior

Consumer behavioral factors influence theory

To research consumer behavior, it has different theory to explain why and how the consumer is influenced to make the choice by different factors. For example, utility theory,it explains that consumers make choices based on the expected outcomes of their decisions. They are viewed as rational decision makers and they only consider self interest.

Utility theory views consumer is as a " rational economic man". However, the factors influence consumer behaviors may include these activities, such as need recognition, information search, evaluation of alternatives, the building of purchase intention , the act of purchasing choice, consumption and finally disposal. Hence, it seems that all the consumer's activities in whose purchase processes. They will influence their choice. For example, when the property purchase consumer , he plans to research different kinds of properties information concern price, location, housing areas, room numbers, building facilities and environment facilities. He will find some sample target properties information to make comparison in order to decide to buy which of property is the most suitable to satisfy his living need.

However, it is not only one activity for the property purchase buyer in his decision making process. It also include evaluation of alternatives activitiy when he ensures the accurate property information number in order to evaluate whether which one of all these property choices is the most suitable one. Hence, it explains that property information research and evaluation of alternatives both activities are needed to spend much time for this property buyer. If he does not plan to find one property to live in short time, it is possible that he can spedn one month, even more than one month or more than three months time to do the only property information gathering activity.

Hence, it seems that time factor is not the main factor to influence the property buyer to do property purchase decision immediately. Otherwise, if the property buyer plans to find one new property to live within one month. Then, time factor is possible one important factor to influence this property purchase chocie decision. For example, if he felt that he needs more time to spend to gather information concerns the large house area size and the properties have more than three bathrooms and/or bedrooms properties information. Then, he will be possible not to find any this kinds of all property information. So, it means that all these properties won't be his choice. It is because long time property information gathering activity factor influnce.

I assume that the property buyer is a economic man and he does not spend much time to do the property information gathering activity. So, this kind of property needs him to spend long time to gather properties inforation in order to make this kind of properties comparison. Moreover, because he expects to live one new property within one month. So, he only chooses the properties, they have less than three bedrooms and/or bathrooms to gather sample properties information in order to make property purchase decision within one month. Hence, the time variable factor can only influence the property purchaser when he/she needs to make decision to buy one new property to live in the short time. If some kinds of properties choices number has a lot and the property buyer feels to let that he/she must need to spend long time to find the suitable properties number to make evaluation alternatives comparison behavior.

Then, the time variable limiting pressure factor will be possible the main factor to influence the property buyer's choice in order to make the most suitable kind of property purchase decision. Hence, it is one case example of how time limiting pressure factor can influence consumer purchase choice decision, such as property purchases market case. The reason explains why the property buyer needs to spend time to do property information gathering. I assume that general property buyer behave rationally in the economic sense. They won't only believe property agent individual property photos advertisement , it concerns where the property location is and facility etc. information on property photos in order to evaluate whether the property price is reasonable to pay. Generally, property buyers need to attempt to gather property information and visit the different actual property locations to make choice. So, general property consumers would have to be aware of all the available different kinds of properties consumptin options from themselves properties information gathering and the properties agents' verbal properties introduction both be capable of correctly rating each property alternative and the available to select the optimum course of the final property purchase action.

Hence, in the property purchase and sold market, limiting time pressure factor will be important influential factor to decide whether the kinds of properties will be option to some property buyers when they feel need to find one suitable property to buy in short time. Otherwise, in some food consumption market , time limiting pressure factor will not be the main factor to influence consumer option. Such utility theory indicates consumers are as one rational economic man, whom do not expect to spend much time to do any options evaluation decision making.

However, in coffee market, buying a coffee comes almost automatically and does not need much information search. Hence, time limiting pressure factor won't one main factor to influence coff consumer to choose to buy the kind of coffee to drink. However, there are other factors to influence coffee consumers' kind of coffee drinking option from cultural, social, personal or psychological factors. So, coffee taste producer can follow these factors to estimate how coffee consumers might behave in the future when making any kinds of coffee making purchasing decisions.

Firstly, social factor can affect coff consumer behavior significantly. Every coffee consumer has someone around influencing his/her coffee buying decisions. The important social factors include reference groups, family, role and status , e.g. when the coffe buyer has high income job and his friends have good educational level and high income. Then, he will compare his reference group, such as his friends' coffee buying behavior choosing which kinds of coffee taste to drink in habits or lifestyles. If he chooses the kind of coffee taste to drink, its price is cheaper to compare his friends' drinking coffee tastes. Then, he may be influenced to follow his friends to drink the same kinds of coffee taste in order to keep their same social status and role between him and his friends.

Secondly, the coffee consumers will be influenced how to choose which kinds tastes of coffee to drink by personal factors, such as his age, life cycle state, occupation, economic situation , lifestyle and personality and self-concept. Age related factors are such as taste in food, e.g. the kinds of coffee taste. Although, coffee price is cheap, but if the coffee consumer's income is more and he/she can often spend to buy different kinds of taste coffees to drink. Then, his/her income level will have much purchasing power to influence his/her purchasing behavior. Hence the coffee consumer's frequency of consumption of different kinds of coffee taste drinking choice behavior will represent whether his/her income level is high or low in possible. For example, the consumer needs to go to automatic coffee shop to buy at least three cups or more different kinds of high class good taste coffee brands to drink per week. Although, these high class coffee brands' prices are higher than the low class of coffee brands. But the coffee consumer still only buys any one of these kinds of high class brands' coffee taste to drink. Hence, it seems that this coffee consumers ought have high income to let hims to buy at least three cups of high class brand of coffee taste to drink from automativ coffee ship per week.

So, income factor can influence the coffee consumer to choose either coffer purchase from supermarket or coffee drinking at automatic coffee shop. If the coffee consumer only chooses to buy coffee from supermarket, due to the bottles of different kinds of brand coffee can provide more different tastes of coffees choices from shelves to let him to buy to drink at home. So, it seems that the coffee consumer's income level is low in general. Otherwise, if the coffee consumer only chooses to go to automtic coffee shop to buy the high class brands of coffee tastes to drink at least thre times or more per week. It may mean that the coffee consumer has high income level to support him/her to often go to automatic coffee shop to buy different kinds of high class coffee tastes to drink frequently every week. Som high or low income level factor can influence every coffee consumer individual drinking coffee behavioral options.

Moreover, when the coffee consumer is younger coffee consumer will be possible to buy much coffee to drink. Because younger age people can accept to drink coffee habitually more than older age people. Also, it is possible that younger peopler feel often drinking coffee behavior will help them to bring more health feeling and /or raising nervous to learn , due to they need often to go to schools to study. Otherwise, older age people feel often drinking coffee behaviors won't help them to bring more health and they do not need to raise nervous to learn.

Finally, even, cultural difference factor will influence coffee consumers number fo any countries. For example, western countries'people like to drink any kinds of coffee tastes traditionally. Asia countries' people like to drink any different kinds of teas tastes traditionally. So, different kinds of teas tastes will be asia people's traditional drinking substitute to replace different kinds of coffee tastes more easily. Hence, culture difference will be one factor to influence asia coffee buyers number. So, it seems that time limiting pressure factor won't influence coffee consumers' coffee taste choices to different kinds of high class or low class brands, visiting coff shops or visiting supermarkets choices, frequent or not frequent coffee drinking behaviors.

How and why time limiting pressure
influences consumer choice

Can consumer buying decisions be influenced by time limiting pressure. For these three situations, they will influence consumer hoe makes different buying decision, e.g. in the little time available, but the consumer needs to do more effort needed to choose to buy which kind of product among variety kinds of product choice or in a moderate amount of time available, or a considerable amount of time available. In this first situation, the consumer can not real attempt to find any weaknesses or unique characteristics of the products, because it has no enough time to allow whom to choose. So, his/her product evaluation won't be th most accurate to satisfy his/her needs because little time can only allow him/her to find some weaknesses of the products. Otherwise, in the final situation, because the consumer has a considerable amout of time to allow him/her to attempt to find the weaknesses and/or strengths characteristics of the products choice. So, he/she ought do the more reasonable or accurate evaluation of these products to choose the most effective economic beneficial product to buy. Thus, it seems that time limiting pressure factor can influence the consumer to make more rational or more reasonable economic beneficial consumption decision making to buy the product or consume the service.

Thus, a consumer buying decision will require these situations to do buying decisions, they may include either little time and conscious effort or a moderate amount of time and effort or a considerable amount time and effort. The products may include cheap products/services , e.g. fruit, DVD, university courses, computers, facial services, surgeries, sport shoes, reference books, soft drinks, magazines as well as expensive products/ services, e.g. cars, houses, luxury goods, e.g. jewellery, female hand bags, holiday travelling entertainment. So, any expensive or cheap products or services, the consumer will need to spend either little or moderate or considerable amount time to do gathering information about the different kinds of products or services in order to find which brand of product or service can bring more economic benefit when he/she chooses to use the product or consume the service. He/she will compare his/her preference sample brands limiting number of products or services choices to decide to buy the brand of product or consume the brand service easily. However in the consumer's consuming decision making process, he/she will need to spend either little or moderate or a considerable amount of time to do the evaluation and choice consumption behavior. It means that time limiting pressure factor will influence the consumer how to make consumption choice consequently.

What are the impacts of reduced branding on consumer choice and time limiting pressure to influence consumer behavior? When one consumer needs to choose products to buy one in a time limiting pressure consumption environment, when branding on packaging is reduced, e.g. the brand of product has 10 different style of packages to let consumer choice, but it reduces to only 5 different style of packages to let consumer choice. How does it influence the consumer decision making when the consumer has little time to allow to choose these 5 different style of packages ? For example, when the consumer expects to spend only 10 minutes to choose any one style of package to buy drom this brand product. Currently, this brand of produxt has reduced different style of packages number from 10 to 5. Do you feel that the consumer will feel easy to do decision making to choose to buy the most attractive style of package product from this brand's 5 different style of packages choices? Is 10 minutes consumption choice time enough to let the consumer to make final purchase decision from these brand's 5 different style of packages choice? Will the time limiting pressure be reduced , due to this brand's 10 style packages are reduced to 5 style packages to let the consumer to choose within the 10 minutes expected limiting consumption choice time.

It is one interesting psychological consumption behavior to research whether the brand's reducing different style of packages number factor will influence the consumer to do the decision making in the short time in the time limiting pressure environment. For toothpaste, shapmo products example, if the brand of these products' style packages choice is reduced to 5 style packages from 10 style packages choice. When one consumer finds the brand of toothpaste or shampo has only 5 style packages on the shelves in supermarket. If the consumer has moderate or considerate amount time to let him/her to choose these both kinds product any one style of packages to buy. The 5 style packages to these both inds of products will be impossible to satisfy the consumer's choice need because he/she haas much time to stay in supermarket to choose. Otherwise, if the consumer has little time to allow to stay in the supermarket , e.g. ony 10 minutes. Then, he/she expects to spend only 10 minutes consumption choice time to do buying decision making within 10 minutes. These both kinds of the brand's products, its styl of packages choice number is reduced to 5, it is possible to satisfy the consumer's choice need to buy this brand of product either toothpaste or shampoo and both of thee brand of products to be chose to buy in the supermarket. So , the reducing style of package number to let consumer choice will be seem to let the conumer to do buying decision making in the limiting time pressure consumption environment.

In fact , package is such a visual to influence consumer decision making in the short time or personal limiting time choice process. If the product has more attractive package design, the it can bring more attention effort to influence the consumer to choose to buy the product in the short time information transfers to influence the consumer decision making to choose to buy more easily , when he/she is active in communication process. So, package, communicating with consumer in the selling place , has become an essential factor to influence the choice of consumer.

Scientific researches have proved that package decisions can attract consumer attention, transfer the desirable information abou tthe product, position , the product in consumer conscious, differentiate and identify of among similar kinds of products. In that way elements of package influence consumer decision making process and can determine the choice of consumer and the package itself can become more competitive advantage.

However it is not absolute that the brand of product has more package choices, it must have more customers to choose to buy its product. For example, there are two brands of shampoo in the supermarket shelf. One brand shampoo has 5 different style of packages and 5 different fruit productive elements to cause similar fresh fruit smells to attract consumers to buy. Another brand shampoo has 3 different style of packages and 3 different fresh fruit smells to attract consumers to buy in the same shelf location also. When one supermarket customer has little time to expect to stay in the supermarket, e.g. he expects only to stay the supermarket maximum to 15 minutes. he expects to buy one bottle shampoo and meats and fruits and vegatables within 15 minutes. Hence, he expects only to spend about 5 minutes to choose one brand of shampoo product as well as he demands to spend maximum 10 minutes to buy other foods within 15 minutes. When he stays in the shampr shelf location, he finds only two brands of shampoo products are displayed on the same shelf location. One brand of shampo has 5 different style packages to let him to choose, but he feels that these 5 diffeent style packages are not very attractive. Otherwise, the another brand of shampo has only 3 different style packages to let him to choose, but he feels that the 3 different style packages are very attractive. Due to he feels time causes pressure to choose these two brands of shampoo immediately. So, he does not want to spend more time more than 5 minutes to choose on brand of shampoo to buy. He will be influenced by the brand of different styles of packages more attraction to influence his buying decision making obviously. So, whether the shampoo brand's package is attractive or not, it will influence the consumer's buying decision making to choose either to buy the brand's shampo product in preference.

So, the more packages choice to the brand's product which may not mean that it has high opportunity to influence consumers' attention. Otherwise, the attractive package element if more important to compare right number of packages choices. Consumer package can influence these elements, e.g. colour, size, imageries, graphics, materials, smell, brand name, producer/country, information, special offers. Of the brand of products can have much attractive elements. Then, it can attract consumers to choose to buy the brand's attractive package products in short time decision making process, such as perception of needs, search for information , evaluation of alternatives, decision making, behavior after purchase. Such as supermarket case, I assume that any supermarket consumers do not expect to spend much time to choose which brand of product is the most suitable or earning more economic benefit to buy when they need to stay the shelf to need spend much time to select which brand of product to buy in the supermarket. Because in general, supermarket consumers ought plan to buy more than one kind of product or food, even more usually. So, limiting time pressure factor will influence their decision making. Similarly, as my explanation indicates why although, the product had attractive package elements and its has many packages number choices, but it does not mean that it can win the similar product which has not more attractive packages, even it has more packages choices number to let supermarket consumers to choose. So, an attractive package element factor will have more influential and potential to cause supermarket consumers to choose to buy it in the supermarket limiting time pressure consumption environment.

CHAPTER TWO

How the time consumption pressure factor influences irrational consumption decision making

When one consumer has a large number of options, he/she will feel time pressure to cause whose accurate and reasonable evaluation. Then, the personal time limiting pressure factor will bring these questions: How does the time limiting pressure influence the consumer evaluation? Will the consumer personal limiting time pressure bring advantages and / or disadvantages in whom consumption decision making? How to help the consumer to solve short time decision problem when he/she encounters extreme time pressure an dchoice overload?

I shall assume every consumer is general one economic man. He/she feels time is important, he /she does not want to spend much time to choose one brand of product to buy among a number of brands of products choices. I also assume that any consumers decision making satisfaction, which is based on search until they found a sufficiently good item, or run not of time. So, it seems that which the consumer needs to buy one kind of product, but the product has a lot number of different brands to let the consumer to choose. The consumer ought need to spend much time to make choice decision making. However, consumer is one economic man, he/she ought not to search all different brands to decide whether which brand of product can bring the much economic value or utility value to choose to buy. So, in general, consumers will only choose sample brands of products to decide to buy the satisfied brand of product. For example, when the consumer needs to buy one television. The television has 20 brands of similar televisions to let he to choose. He will not spend much time to search these similar 20 televisions information. He will only gather sample 10 to 15 or less different brands of televisions to compare what their strengths and weaknesses, unique characteristics. Then, he will make decision to choose to buy the best television from these sample televisions. Hence, in general, consumers will feel time pressure when they feel need to spend much time to choose a lot different brands of similar products. Because they feel time is not enough to let they can do other important matters when they need to spend much time to do search information behavior when they need to buy any products ususally. Hence, it is general consumers psychology that they will feel real choice under time pressure and choice overload, when they have too much a lot of similar brands of products to let them have opportunity to choose to make decision making to buy only one brand of product.

However, when a brand of product is familiar and given its simplicity and familiarity to general consumers' acknowledgement. It will have perference advantage to attract or influence consumers' attention or consideration. So, when the market has similar different brands of products are available to let consumers to choose. The largest choice set is not large enough to create overload to influence the brand's sale when consumers need to spend much time to choose these different brands similar products to buy. Because when the brand's any products are familiar and given its simplicity and familiarity to general consumers' knowledgement. Then, it can build utility confidence to influence general consumers , it will be preference sample brand of product to do buying making option. Hence, the brand's familiarity factor will influence general consumers' preference buying decision making option. So, any product manufacturers need to concern how to build its brand familiarity to let many consumers to acknowledge in order to raise its competitive effort. Raising brand's familiarity may be a good method to solve consumer individual choice under time pressure overload , because when the brand of product is preference sample brand to any consumers. It's sale opportunity will also be raised. So, it brings the question: How can the brand of products can cause general consumers' preference choice. For food example, food brands were more likely to choose the implicitly preferred brand over the explicitly preferred one when choices were made under time pressure.

Imagining one customer enters a supermarket 10 minutes before closing time. He failed to write up a shopping list. So, when the staff is preparing to close store at the night, the consumer hurry trys not to for set too many of the ingredients for dinner . What brands of products , he opts for, as he can choose from a variety of similar foods, but time is short and the staff is looking at the consumer impatienty? It is possible that the consumer will probably quickly decide in favor of the foods he likes best, pay, and leave the evening.

Hence, supermarket consumer's first time feeling to the brand of food will influence whom choice. One target category and one attribute category share same response key: Pleasant vs unpleasant feeing, if the supermarket consumer has pleasant feeling when he sees the food photos and touchs the package of the brand of food to feel pleasant in the short supermarket closing time. Then, his pleasant feeling will be chooses to buy the brand of food to eat. Thus, the consumer individual pleasant or unpleasant feeling factor will influence whom consumption choice, such as this supermarket closing time pressure consumption.

In fact, many factors may influence whether consumer behavior is under more or less control. Hunger may influence control in the domain of eating behavior

. So, such as the supermarket will close soon,it has store closing time pressure to influence the consumer needs hurry to make choice decision to buy food. If the consumer feels more hungry, he will not spend much time to find the right food to buy. He will be influenced by the different brand's food packages whether which brand of food package can bring a more pleasant to let him to feel, when he touchs and sees the brand of food package. He won't spend time to search whether the different kinds of brands of foods have how much different health elements because the supermarket will close store soon. So, he only depends his individual pleasant feeling to make final food purchase decision. If he feels all of the kinds of brands foods are unpleasant food packages when he sees and touchs them first time as well as he does not feel much hungry. Then, it is possible that he won't choose to any one food to eat. He will choose to go to restaurant to get dinner to replace buying food to cook to eat dinner at home at the night.

The another case is that time pressure concerns how on choice of information source impacts purchase decisions. When the consumer who buys one product , he needs to use the same number of information sources to search the product's information regardless of time pressure. Because he has more available time, he devotes more time , but only to selected the right sources to search information about the product. He will mostly use marketing dominant sources, e.g. magazine. he feels magazine can give more accurate information concerns to the product's good or bad quality real more reasonable and fair evaluation to let the consumer to acknowledge. so, when the consumer has much time to choose to buy which brand of product is the most best choice. He will buy magazine to find information. He believes magazine has more fair evaluation to different brands of product. It won't mislead consumers to make wrong decision making. Hence, in general, when consumers have much time to find information source to search which brand of product is more value to buy. They will attempt to buy consumer magazine to acknowledge whether the different brands of product , which have unique characteristics, strengths or weaknesses in order to compare them to make more accurate evaluation to choose to buy which brand of the kind product. When they have no time pressure to influence their choice process time to be shortened or reduced. Otherwise, these consumers will depend on newspapers, television, radio advertisments information sources when they feel time pressure controls their consumption choice decision making process time to be shortened or reduced. Hence, time pressure will be possible to influence consumer individual information source channel choice.

Time pressure consumption decision
making process characteristics

How we can predict or know the consumer time pressure in whom decision making process? Will it bring advantages or disadvantages to influence the businessmens' benefits? I shall indicate some different consumption situations or environments to explain what will be impacted to sale number is increased or decreased to businesses when the consumer feel time pressure to avoid whom behavioral consumption to the product or the service.

Firstly, I shall explain that what effects of product popularity and time pressure on online shopping behaviors are . Electronic ecommerce is popular to any countries, in special, US, UK, China large areas countries, because when one customer feels need to spend one hour even more time to catch any transportation tool to arrive the shop to buy the kind of product. Then, due to far distance reason, he/she will choose to apply internet to buy the kind of product . If the seller has website to let the consumers to choose online shopping. However, it seems that online shopping behavior can reduce the consumer individual time pressure, when he/she feels need to catch any kinds of transportation tool to arrive the shop to buy the product. Moreover, when the consumer can turn on home computer to enter its website to choose the styles of the kind of products, which one is the most situable to choose. He/she can spend time to search the different styles kinds of product information to compare and evaluate which brand of product will b whose purchase choice easily at home.

Hence, in psychological view, he/she can feel that spending time to search information from internet behavior which is more valuable and it can bring more economic benefit to make final purchase decision more than the behavior of spending long time to catch any transportation tools to visit the shop. Moreover, it is possible to bring failure risk that he/she wastes time to catch any transportation tools to visit the shop if he/she can not find any one of suitable product(s) to choose to buy. Hence, it seems the online shopping can influence the consumer reduced time pressure and wastes time to do any shopping decision.

This is online shopping's attractive strengths to the consumers when they need to spend long time to catch any kinds of transportation tools to visit the shop or when the consumer feels hurry to do other important matters, he/she can not allow himself/herself to spend long time to do his/her visiting the shop behavior. Moreover, another online shopping's advantage is that product popularity can be perceived by examining the information presended on websites. For example, research on onlin reviews confirms the review quantity presented with products become positively influences to consumers' purchase intention and it can persuade the online visitor can make decision to buy the product when he/she has enter the seller's online website to find the most suitable product to choose to buy more easily. Hence, it seems that it is more easy to persuade the online visitor to make final purchase decision more than visiting the shop , when the online visitor can attempt to do the click mouse behavior to enter the seller's online shop, such as website. Then, he/she will be influenced to view the seller's different kinds of colourful and attractive product pictures from the seller's wesite.

Consequently, it has much opportunity to persuade the consumer to do the final purchase decision. if the seller's website is attractive to persuade him/her to visit its website to find any new products more than five times, even tem times or every weak several times , even day one time frequently visiting behavior from internet channel. Hence, due to internet is convenient tool to let consumers to find any product informatons from the seller's website at home or public library , computer, or mobile phone. Consumers must find any product informations any time in any places easily. So, online shopping can reduce any consumers' time pressure to visit any shops to expect to achieve final consumption decision aim in possible. Thus, it seems that online shopping method can influence consumers to feel time saving and time presure reducing consumption both advantages more than visiting shops' shopping method when the consumer is living far away from the shop. When the consumer feels that he/she is experiencing situational time pressure, then, he/she will respond well to seek another time saving situational consumption environment. So , it explains when one consumer feels he/she has no much time to catch long time transportation tool to visit the shop on the day. When he/she has computer at home, he/she will attempt to type the shop name to research whether it has online shopping platform service from internet. Because he/she does not want to spend one hour, even more time to catch transportation tool to arrive the shop, when he/she can't walk to the shop in short time. Even, he/she may feel online shopping behavior won't influence his/her eating , sleeping, or recreational time to be reduced at home or any places , when he/she can behave the online shopping behavior at home or any where conveniently. Consequently, promoting online shopping is as a time-saver is likely to be effective for these experiencing situational time pressure. Those with situational pressure would almost certainly welcome anything that would reduce their activity level and the demands on their time. In fact, there is really no adult learning method for store shopping because it is something everyone learns to do from early childhood. But for many adult consumers, they feel have interest to learn how to use internet and web to shopping. Some adult will feel interest and it is value to learn how to use internet channel to anticipate the complexity of shopping online. For example, Super Walmart cheap frocery store that carries many thousands of products and brands to let online shoppers won't feel confused when viewing its online merchant's home page with only a few menu items and links from its website. So, Super Walmart website can let online shoppers to feel difficult that they can save much time to enter any merchants' home page . They only need to view the Super Walmart's website ,then they can find any preference cheap grocercies to compare and evaluate which one(s) is (are) value to buy. So, Super Walmart's website can let global cheap grocery online shoppers feel it can help them to save time to find any merchant's products from internet conveniently. Consequently, online shopping will be one popular time saving consumption channel to reduce time pressure to some consumers nowadays.

Secondly, I shall explain that what determines purchase decisions for airline tickets when the traveller fees time stress. When a travelling planner has no enough time to prepare whose travelling journey, whether the time stress will influence he/she feels decision difficulties and frustration, when it will cause he/she needs to gather significant amounts of information to lead to make to choose which airline ticket is the most right choice? How and number of airline options and time pressure influence the airline ticket buyer's purchase decision?

However, there are both kinds of time pressures to influence the airline ticket buyer's airline choice decision, they focus on either real decision deadlines (physical time), such as the journey beginning day is any day of this week or tomorrow or subjective feeling of pressure with time (sense of urgency or psychological time), such as the traveller expects that he/she fears all airlines' all seats are full booked in this month. Moreover, he/she can plan to catch air plane to travel next month. So, he/she will attempt to gather any airlines' tickets prices, flight day and time and destination arrival and weather information in this month to avoid that it is too late to delay his/her next month travelling plan.

Hence, it seems that the effect of number of airlines choices and air tickets purchase deadlines (physical time limit) will influence how the traveller or air ticket buyer's purchase decision using secondary data to search of airline ticket. for example, if the traveller felt time is no enough to let him/her to go to travel agent to enquire any airlines' air tickets prices and seats and date and time air plan departure available time to concern the traveller's destination choice. Then, he/she will be probable to choose to buy electronic-ticket (e-ticket) from internet. If he/she has computer to link internet to gather any airlines' flying date and time and seat available information at home easily. Hence, it seems that one time pressure traveller will be probable to choose e-ticket purchase at home in preference. If the airline can provide online e-ticket purchase option to the time pressure traveller. Due to the pressure time traveller feels closer to departure, the negative impact of number of airline options is not as strong when he/she can view the airline's website to find the flight date, time and seat available information to purchase e-ticket to prebook the date and time to departure the traveller's country and to arrive his/her travelling destination information from the airline's website channel at home or anywhere any time conveniently. Hence, travel agency can bring a positive relationship between airline number of options and pre-booking airline that immediate possibility. When the time pressure traveller hopes the airline can build the good interactive relationship between number of options and decision time limit (number of days till planned travel effort on e-ticket purchase probabilities. So, if the airline website can let the traveller to predict when date and time is accurate available to arrive whom frequently destination choice country as well as the e-ticket's real price , it is not e-ticket preductive price and the real seats number available, it is not the estimated seats number available on the departure time and date to the travelling or arrival country destination. Then, all of these online information to the airline, which will raise the e-ticket pre-booking purchase chance to let the e-ticket buyer to make whose final e-ticket purchase choice decisin to win its e-ticket competitors easily.

Consequently, a real time e-ticket information can attract any time pressure e-ticket buyers to choose to buy its e-ticket (electronic airline ticket) more than visiting travel agent's paper airline ticket option when the travel feels hurry to buy airline ticket to travel in short time.

CHAPTER THREE

Reducing time pressure consumption methods

How can sellers persuade consumers to choose to buy their products or consume their services in time pressure environment easily? It is a valuble research topic to concern how to know how consumer individual decision making to spend his/her available resources (time, money and efforts, or consumption relatd aspects) as well as how any why he/she chooses the preference brand to buy its any kind of products or consume its services, when he/she chooses to buy the brand of products or consume its services? Hence, marketers need to obtain an indepth knowledge of consumer buying behavior.

In any buying process, time factor will have about 10 % to 40 % to influence consumer decision. When the consumer feels hurry to consume, e.g. planning to go to travel, when he/she needs to choose to buy which airline's air ticket and what day and time is the right air ticket prebooking purchase decision right time choice; or enrolling which school to be choosed course to study decison, e.g. how long time is needed to be choose which school is the most suitable to provide the most suitable courses studying choce change; purchase warm clothes to wear in winter, when is the suitable time to choose to buy the cheaper warm clothers to prepare to wear in winter, e.g. Jan to Mar., April to June, July to Aug. month; when is the most suitable time to buy another new house to live, when the property consumer(buyer) has lived present house for long time, e.g. three years or more. All of these issues will include time factor to influence the consumer feels when he/she ought choose to buy the kind of product or consume the kind of service. However, the other factors will also include to influence his/her decision, e.g. family, friend relationship factor, advertising factor, social status factor, cultural difference factor, personal psychological need level or satisfactory level factor, young or old age factor, income level factor, economic environment factor, material enjoyable need factor etc. factors. However, time pressure factor will be the consumer individual intrinsic (internal) psychological feeling factor, and it is the consumer individual intrinsic feeling to judge whether when he/she ought spend some money to buy the kind ofcnew product or the kind of consume service (what time is the most reasonable or the most suitable time) to make purchase choice decision. However, when the consumer feels hurry to make purchase decision. So, he/she will not hope to spend more time to gather more information to compare and evaluate which one is the right brand of product tochoose to buy or the right service to consume among different brands of products or services. Otherwise, if the consumer has more time or he/she can make the decision to buy any brand of product. Then, he/she ought spend more time to gather more information to compare and evaluate which one is the most suitable product choice to buy or which one is the right service choice to consume. So, time pressure factor will have some influence to any consumers to make decision about what time is the suitable time to buy the kind of product or consume the service. For example, heater product is usually when winter weather time, the heater products need number ought increase in winter weather time or season. But, it is possible that the heater products need number won't increase in winter season / weather possible, when one country , there are many householders or families , they have one heater number at least at home. Then, it is possible that these householders or families won't have consumption desires to buy one more heater product to use in winter at home, because they have had one heater to use at home in winter. So , when the country has have many customers number, they are using the kind of heater products at homes. Most people own at least one heater number factor will have possible to influence enough time available to cause they do not feel hurry to buy any heaters to use at homes, so, their do not feel time pressure to buy any heaters in short time. Because they do not plan to buy the kind of product to use at home in short time when they have one heater product at least to use at homes in present.

Hence, it brings this question: How to attract or persuade the customers, they are using the kind of product to let they feel time pressure to make decision to buy another new or same brand of product to replace to use? The product's better quality , long durable time useful, brand loyalty and past good purchase experience factors will influence him/her to feel time pressure to need to buy another new product in short time. So,when the consumer feel time pressure to make decision to purchase, he/she will choose when is the most right time to gather information, search, select, use and dispose of another new product to replace the old product in the short time.

Hence, the brand of product needs have good product motives, may be raised to the consumer's impluse, desires, considerations which make the buyer purchase the brand's new product to replace the present using product in order to achieve whose satisfactory needs to emotional product motives and rational product motives both. Moreover, persuading or encouraging the consumer feels he/she has real need to buy the kind of new product or replace the present old product (s), the brand of product marketer needs let the consumer feels these any one of nature of motive to raise his/her purchase decision desire in time pressure environment. The natures of motive may include: When the consumer feels desire for saving money, he/she will choose to buy it when the brand of product falls down, when he/she feels fear to be sickness, retirement, he/she will choose to buy insurance policy, when he/she feels pride, or high social status knowledgement, he/she will buy premium product , e.g. gold, expensive watch, car , when he/she feels fashion need, he/she will move house to live from rural to urban, or rural people imitate urban to learn to do their fashion living behavior, when he/she feels possession need, he/she will feel need to buy antiques for its future unique worth satisfactory feeling in possible, when he/she feels health need, he/she will choose to buy health foods, join memebership in health clubs, when he/she needs to enjoy comfortable feeling, he/she will feel need to buy micro-oven, washing machine to use at home, when he/she feels love and affection need, he/she will buy gift items to give to whose friends or families for presents in their birthday or lover day etc. special days to let they to feel happy. So, when the marketer can touch the consumer individual different nature of motives to satisfy his/her personal purchase feeling need and it can know how to influence them to feel that they have these any one of purchase motive needs in short time. Then, they will be persuaded to raise time pressure to make purchase decison to buy any kind of products in short time.

However, instead of attractive good product quality method can attempt consumers to make time pressure consumption behavior. The another method is brand loyalty building method, which can be attempted to encourage or persuade consumers to feel consumption desire need to make decision to buy the brand of any products in time pressure consumption environment. For example, when the consumers feel the brand is loyalty and it can build good image to his/her feeling , and this time pressure factor can inlfuence this brand of any products which has high discount price to attract the consumer individual attention , e.g. familiar brand high class cars, the good confident house agent's high class houses, and the expensive and infrequently buying items, come under this category. When their prices are fallen down to sell cheaper , e.g. twenty per cent discount or more than twenty percent discount sale price than the other similar competitive brands' any products' normal prices. Then, it is possible to let these expensive items' consumers have high involvement and high feeling need in time pressure consumption environment. Because they assume that this discount sale price will be short time sale price, e.g. after three months or next month etc. short time discount sale price in short time period. Then, these expensive items' prices will be raised to the normal sale price, even higher price. so, they have time pressure feeling to feel that it is right time to make consumption decision in order to avoid to lose these low price purchase benefit in this unpredictive cheap discount price purchase items. so, if the expensive item marketer can build long time good brand loyalty relationship to consumers. Then, it will have much influential effort to persuade consumers feel consumption desires need by its any extensive items in the unpredictive short term discount period, due to they do not want to loss this large discount purchase price chance. So, short time discounted sale price, it is another method to persuade consumers to choose to buy the brand's any products in short time pressure consumption environment.

The another persuading time pressure consumption method is that it can let consumers to think more habitual buying the kind of products. products like stationery, groceries, food etc. fall under this category. For example, when the consumer fees the brand of any products ,he/she has habitual purchase experience, of he/she feels that the brand's any products won't sell in market temporary, even he/she can not buy it to use again. Then, it is possible to infuence him/her to feel immediate purchase need to buy a lot of product or food number to keep to use or eat later in the time pressure environment, e.g. the food consumer buys the brand of any breads to eat in supermarkets habitually, but in this moth, he/she watchs TV advertisement to be acknowledge this brand of any breads won't be bought from any supermarkets as soon as possible. Hence, it is possible to influence him/

her to plan to make choice to buy a lot of number of this brand of any breads in order to keep the enough of this brand of breads number to eat later. So, this brand of any breads sale loss in supermarkets that will cause the habitual food consumers of this brand of breads, whom make consumption choice to buy a lot number of this brands any breads in short time suddenly. Because they are eating this brand of any kinds of breads habitually. They feel much eating need to lot number of this brand of any breads in short period, because it can satisfy their habitual taste needs of this brand's any kinds of breads. So, brand loyalty and habitual consumption to the kind of product or food , ehich will result simply from the habit and it can influence the consumers feel consumption need to buy the brand's any kinds of products or foods when they feel that they may not buy it again or they can not earn discount advantage after the short time. So, any one of these sale strategies will have possible to raise the consumer individual consumption desire to the brand of products in the short time pressure consumption environment. Also it needs to spend much time to gather information in order to make purchase decision, because the brand had built confidence to consumers when they feel this brand's any products or foods are better to compare the similar brands' any products or foods habitually. So, time pressure consumption environment will persuade them to feel consumption desire to buy this brand's any products or foods in short time. When, they fer that they can not buy any more for this brand's any kinds of products or foods or discounting price in this final short purchase time.

In conclusion, these factors can influence consumer behaviors to be changed to feel time pressure need to do purchase decision making behavior from encough time gathering information available feeling behavior. They have these same views, e.g. habits and routines are very influential, particularly for behaviors repeated daily in a semi-automatic fashion. The consumer's past purchas experience to the brand's products, positive or negative emotion to the brand's products, and the brand's familization, recognition are strong influence , the information available , it is the consumer's mind and the relative important information given to let the consumer knows form different advertisement medias matters for decision making, greating between pieces of information and can be influenced by personal psychological timing limited pressure, the consumer's comparison to differences in price or other characteristics, many pursue value (or in bargain), and compare to alternatives or past knowledge, consumer personal greater value on the immediate future and heavily disocunt future costs or savings to the brand of product, feeling simple and easy decision making process to the product , it can lead the consumer to avoid to spend long time to make purchasing decision and the consumer will easy to choose to buy the product when he/she feels have a loss value if he/she does not decide to buy the product in the short time. SO, it seems that when the marketer can motivate the consumer's consumption desire to feel saving money, promote health, avoid waste time and less nervous workload to gather information for comparison and evaluation alternatives aim. It is seen favorably by the consumer personal time pressure purchase decision making and sense of justice influence factors.

However, sociologists have categorised the motives for consumption behaviors in the short time by the fundamental consumption decision making needs or wants which they satisfy, e.g. having a clear understanding what benefits, characteristics, economic value to the brand's any products , feeling consumption decision making process is a leisure activity. These drivers for consumption behaviorw will either bring positive or negative to influence the consumer personal emotion, either owning enough time available or time pressure environmental impacts can be seen to influence whether the consumer feels he/she needs how long time to be spent to make comparison and evaluate alternatives in order to make final purchase choice in whom decision making process. Hence, the consumer himself/herself time pressure consumption decision making feeling, it can bring positive purchase choice influence,when the marketer can build brand loyalty to let many consumers to feel in the market. Otherwise, if the marketer can not build brand loyalty to let many consumers to feel, but consumers feel time pressure to compare and evaluate its any products to other similar brands of products in the competitive market. Then, its products may be not the preference choices the many customers among the different brands of products choices. So, building long time brand loyalty relationship to satisfy consumers' needs, it will bring positive preference purchase choice to raise the sale effort to the brand of any products when consumers need to make purchase choice in time pressure consumption environment, e.g. seasonal discount sale period, products or foods shortage supply period, without any forever sale possibility in market. Hence , it seems that brand loyalty building factor will influence any brands of products /foods /service sale or provison number to be raised or reduced in possible. Also, it can explain why and how it has close cause and effect relationship between time pressure consumption environment and the brand loyalty building to the brand of products/foods/services to any marketers nowadays.

What are the in-store and out-store
factors influence supermarket
fast moving consumer decision

It is one interesting question: How can the brand of product seller influence the supermarket/store fast-moving consumers' more visual attention when the supermarket/store visitor is hurry to make decision to choose to buy which brand of product in time pressure environment? Supermarket/store fast-moving consumers do not usually spend much time to say in any supermarket shelf locations to choose numerous similar alternative brands of products. However, I assume the fast-moving supermarket/store consumer's decision is dependent on the interaction between the supermarket different shelf location sale environment and the mind of the consumer. So, the eye tracking explores this rapid processing that lacks conscious access or control to any supermarket or store consumers.

It brings this question: How product packing and placement (as in-store factors) and recognition, preferences, and choice task (as out-of-store factors) which will influence the supermarket / store consumer individual decision making process through visual attention. In split-second decision making, the ability to recognize and comprehend a brand of supermarket/ store product can significantly impact preferences. Hence, how the supermarket/store consumer's eye truly sees what whom mind is prepared to influence how much consumption desire to choose to buy the brand's product in short tim decision making process when he/she stays in the shelf location, it has less than ten or more than ten different kinds of brands products or foods to let the visitor to choose in the supermarket or store.

Brand owners and product developers will feel responsibilities to overcome promotion or advertising or communicaton challenge in order to let consumers to know their products are launched on the market. However, it is not until the product reaches the supermarket shelf that has good quality to the effort is judged whether it has how much sale number every day in the supermarket. The judges are the consumers themselves how to make decision quickly through the personal time pressure environment with minor package information processing in the supermarket.

What does it take to be consider an option to influence the consumers' minds on visual attention in point-of-purchase decision making ? The supermarket's in-store activities and the consumer personal out-of-store activities will influence how his / her visual attention to the brand of products in the supermarket / store any shelf locations when he/she is walking to pass any shelf locations. So, it seems that any supermarkets or stores brands of products sale number , it has relation to every supermarket or store visitors' visual attention throughout the point to point (shelf to shelf) decision making process in the supermarkets / stores. So, how much does the supermarket's visitors' time spending to obtain attention to the brand of produc? it will have possible to influence the brand of any products' sale number in the supermarket/store. Hence, in this limited timeframe, the consumer enters a decision making process that is in itself influenced by in-store and out-of-store both factors.

I shall explain what is supermarket / store space quality factor, e.g. top level versus floor level to different shelf variable height, weigh , or shelf space location factor as well as the product price elasticity and price-quality relationship to the brand of products both factors to influence every consumer decision making in supermarket/store. The in-store factor is more influential factor to compare out-of-store factor to influence consumers' decision in supermarket. For example, where the shampoo brand products are locating to be put on the shelf , it can influence the point to point behavior of shampoo product habitual buyers. If the buyer habitually chooses the shampoo brand products in the shelf location. Also, if all of the shampoo brand products are moved to another shelf locations to display its different kinds of shampoo products to cause the habitual buyer needs to spend much extra time to find where the another new shelf location is displaying the brand's shampoo products.

In this situation, information processing has a heightened decision making role as the buyer needs to spend much time to find where the brand's displayed shampoo products' shelf location to make non-habitual decision making between options. For habitual decisons, the consumer's visual attention is reduced to measuring visual search. However, when the brands of any shampoo products are moved to another new shelf location to display its different kinds of shampoo products. So, the act of another shelf new location search , it will influence the habitual shampoo buyer's visual attention to consider the brand of any shampoo products which are usually used to wash to his/her hair habitually. When he / she can find the other new brands of shampoo products are displayed on the old shelf displayed location of the brand of shampoo products. Hence, the traditional shelf displayed location to the brand of products, when the brand of products are moved to another new displayed shelf locations. This in-store factors that will influence traditional cosnumers through visual attention concerns to this brand of products more or less.

So, supermarket traditional shelf displayed variable location to the brand of products factor, which will have influence to the traditional consumers' visual attention to do either buying the brand's products or buying another brand's products to replace it, when the traditional consumer feels difficult that he/she needs to spend extra longer time to find whether where is the traditional useful product's displayed shelf location. Then, it will be possible to influence the traditional consumer's traditional purchase decision to the brand's product, and he/she will choose to buy another brand of product to replace when it can be displayed to the shelf location to attract the consumer's visual attention more.

It is one important in-store shelf displayed factor to influence the traditional fast-moving consumer individual purchase decision making behavioral change in any supermarkets or stores when they feel hurry to do personal time pressure consumption decision to make purchase final decision in the point to point counter purchase (the brand's of products are moved from the traditional shelf location visual attention moves to the strange shelf location visual attention) in supermarket time pressure consumption environment.

Hence, in supermarket time pressure consumption environment, in -store and out-of-sore both factors can influence fast-moving consumer individual purchase decision making. The in-store factors can influence product packaging, product placement components as well as the out-store factors can influence choice task, preference and brand recognition components. So, it is common to influence supermarket consumers choose do personal time pressure purchase consumption decision of visual attention purchase behaviors. The different brands' products are displayed to different shelf locations in order to cause shelf displaying products' different decision making effect.

However, instead of shelf displaying location factor, package will also influence consumers' decision making, due to the influence of minute differences in packaging design on visual attention. When, the supermarket consumer feels the brands are not familiar or unfamiliar. Then, he/she will spend more time to evaluate and verify the unfamiliar brands' products whether which one is value to buy in her/his decision making process. He/she will feel visual attention need in order to evaluate in set of brand alternatives to make conscious demand mind cognitive effort by involving working memory. So, if the product's package is attractive, even the consumer is unfamiliar the brand's any product choices which are displayed on the shelf location in the supermarket. The brand's attractive package factor can influence the consumer to raise whom visual attention. Then, the attractive package factor can increase much visual attention chance to many consumers when they are walking to pass through the unfamiliar brand's any products' shelf displaying location considerably. So, it explains when attractive package factor may solve the visual attention problem to fast-moving consumers when they are visiting one strange supermarket to find anywhere unfamiliar brand's products' shelf displaying locations. Because they are the non-traditional consumers to the unfamiliar brand's products, they won't be influenced to choose either buying or not buying the unfamiliar brand's products. When the unfamiliar brand's products are moved to another new shelf displayed location. So, if the unfamiliar brand has attractive package to let the non-traditional consumers feel visual attention when they are passing through the strange shelf displayed location. Then, it can raise purchase chance to the non-traditional consumers target number when they are staying in the strange supermarket. In conclusion, the brand of products' shelf displaying location and package factors may bring much influence to any traditonal or non-traditonal consumer behaviors in supermarket or store time pressure consumption environment.

CHAPTER FOUR

What consumption is most influenced in preference choice by time pressure

What kinds of services or products are most influenced to consumer behavioral change by time pressure? Can time pressure factor influence more preference to other factors, such as age, culture, income level, habitual shopping, family or friend relationship etc. factors to influence consumer behavioral choice to these kinds of services or products in consumption market? I shall indicate some kinds of services or products consumption models to explain how time pressure can influence consumers to choose to consume its services or buy its products.

Firstly, for theme park entertainment industry example, has it time pressure to cause any theme park visitors, e.g. Walt Disney entertainment theme park to influence them to feel time pressure to enjoy their emotions to play any entertainment machine facilities and it brings negative emotion to choose the entertainment theme park entertainment consumption activities.

For Walt Disney entetainment theme park example, every visitor needs to pay a fixed ticket fee to enter Disney theme park. So, however, he/she chooses to play how many number of entertainment activities facilities, e.g. only one entertainment playing facility, or more than one entertainment playing facilities. The Disney visitor needs to pay the same ticket fee to enter Disney. So, it will cause th visitors feel unfair , they do not choose to play any entertainment facilities or play only less number of entertainment facilities. Because they need to pay the same ticket price to same to the visitors, who choose to play many entertainment facilities number in Disney. So, it brings this question: Does the Disney visitor feel time pressure when he/she chooses to play many number of entertainment facilities , but he/she will not enjoy to carry on other activities in Disney, e.g. shopping, visiting cinema to watch movies, walking around the whole Disney anywhere to view scene activities. Because US Disney entertainment theme park is very large . It has not only entertainment facilities to attract visitors to play. It has many places are value to visitors to visit or enjoy the other free charge entertainment activities , such as visiting Disney gardens, visiting ocean park, visiting Disney cinema to watch free movies, view scene or seeing free charge ocean animal performance shows , going to Disney shopping centres to shopping, visiting Disney library to read books, visiting Disney ocean park to view different kinds of beautiful fishes non-entertainment machine facility playing activities. All of these activities are value to any Disney visitors to choose to play or visit, instead of entertainment machine facilities activities. So, if one visitor hopes only to spend one day in US Walt Disney entertainment theme park. He/she will feel hurry to choose to play any machine entertainment facilities, or he/she won't choose any machine entertainment facilities to play in Disney because he/she also hopes to play other non-machine entertainment facilities activities, e.g. visiting garden, visiting ocean park, visiting library, visiting cinema to watch free movies, visiting garden to play free charge boats water entertainment activities, watching ocean animal show performance etc. different kinds of entertainment activities, even walking around anywhere fun and excite places in Disney theme park. Hence, the Disney visitor will feel time pressure to choose either playing any kinds of entertainment machine facilities or visiting different places in the whole one day in Disney.

Hence, time pressure factor may influence any one of Disney visitors how to choose any entertainment activities to spedn time in Disney. It will bring this question: Because the Disney ticket price is fixed fee, can the Disney visitor will feel unfair to cause negative emotion, if the Disney visitor feels time pressure to choose to play any kinds of machine entertainment activities or doing other non-machine entertainment activities in the Disney visitor's limited timeframe, during he/she stays in Disney? So, it seems that time pressure psychological factor will may influence some Disney visitors to feel unhappy, negative emotion, when they feel their entertainment activities choices are wrong or doing wring entertainment decision making in his/her limited timeframe. Consequently, time pressure factor will influence some feeling time pressure Disney visitors won't choose to enter

Disney again. Hence, time pressure factor can have much influence to theme park visitors' behavioral change, instead of whether the entertainment theme park's machine entertainment facilities are attractive or enjoyable playing or how many entertainment facilities are supplied to let visitors to play in the entertainment theme park. So, entertainment theme park service providerd need to consider whether their ticket prices are reasonable to let visitors feel, if they do not want to reduce theme park visitors number seriously.

The another example is restaurant food service industry. Can time pressure influence food consumers to choose the restaurant to eat? Instead of food taste, price, seats available providing, restaurant location, public transportation facilities available etc. factors, which can influence the food consumer individual choice to the restaurant.

Is time pressure another one main factor to influence food consumers choice to the restaurant? In what suitation, food consumers will feel time pressure to influence whose preference restaurant choice? I assume that the restaurant 's price is reasonable, public transportation facility is convenient to catch to go to the restaurant, food taste is acceptable to the food consumer. Although all above these factors are accepted to the food consumer . But when the food consumer feels hurry to hope to find one restaurant to eat and he/she hopes to spend less time to sit down to eat in the restaurant , e.g. less than one hour. Then, the food consumer will compare all the restaurants are near to whose working place or school , if he/she is one student or one working person. Because he/she needs to eat lunch to go to school or go to office to work. So, the restaurant's food taste, price is not the main factor to influence him/her to choose to eat. Otherwise, whether the restaurant needs him/her to spend how long queue time to wait, or/and the restaurant needs how long cooking time to let him/her to eat, the restaurant needs him/her to walk how long time to arrive the restaurant. All of these factors concern " efficient cooking time, queue waiting time serice performance" issues to the restaurant, which are the main evaluation requirements to influence the feeling time pressure food consumer to make decision whether he/she either still ought follow the better food taste, cheap food price factors to be preference decision or he/she ought follow short time queue time waiting or without queue time waiting, fast cooking waiting time factors to be preference restaurant consumption decision.

Hence, it seems that a feeling time pressure food consumer, he/she ought choose the restaurant to eat in preference when it does not need him/her to wait long queue time and wait long cooking time. Otherwise, when the food consumer does not feel hurry to eat, he/she outhgt choose the restaurant, it can provide good taste food, cheap price in preference to eat.

Hence, time pressure personal feeling will influence students or working people food consumers' preference restaurant choice when the restaurant can provide short time queue waiting or without queue waiting and fast cooking time service preference to satisfy their needs.

However , in some situation, time pressure can influence consumers to choose the service, even its price is expensive than other services. For example, public transportation tool choices service. When one passenger has need to find one kind public transportation tool to catch from the place to another destination, but the destination is far away from his/her location. He/she hopes to catch the kind of public transportation tool to arrive the destination about one hour. Although, his/her location has cheap public transportation tools to choose, e.g. bus, train, tram, ferry, underground train. But, he/she feels that all of these public transpotation tools need to spend longer time to compare taxi to arrive the destination. Although, these public transportation tools can be possible to arrive the destination withing one houe and they must charge cheaper fee to compare taxi. But, however the passenge hopes to arrive the destination in the shortest time. The most important influential factor is that the passenger feels personal time pressure to need to arrive the destination fastly and taxi public transportation tool is believed the fast transportation tool to arrive any destination to compare other general public transportation tools , when it has no traffic jam external environment factor influence. So, time pressure factor will influence passenger to choose taxi transportation tool in preference. Also, it seems that when the place often has many time pressure passengers are living. Then, the place's taxi business will be possible better than other locations. Hence, it implies that time pressure factor will bring need or demand number to be increased to some services.

Time pressure also influences how consumers choose to buy the kind of product, when he/she feels that the kind of product will be old fashin or it is not popular to use in society. For example, computer product, the traditional desktop large heavy weight computers will be possible to be replaced to use at home or office or any building places. Due to the laptop small light weight computers , it can be brought to anywhere by the users easily, even it can be brought to catch public transportation tool to use, it can be brought to restaurant, library, shopping centre etc. different public places to use conveniently. Due to some working people feel hurry to use computer to do their tasks, e.g. typing one document in short time. If they are not working in office and they have no computer on hand. They will worry about that they can not finish their tasks to give their bosses in limited time on the working day.

Hence, laptop computer will be one good chocie of task tool for busy working people when they need to often to use computer to finish urgent tasks in any time. Hence, it seems that the feeling time pressure working people will choose laptop computer in preference more than desktop traditional computer working tool. Due to the feeling time pressure workers, they feel that they can not finish their daily tasks in office. So, they will feel to need to use laptop computer task tool to help them to do office tasks . When they are catching transportation tool to go home or office time or lunch time , or holiday time. So, laptop computer product is more popular to time pressure working people target consumers.

Laptop computer products can also increase the feeling time pressure student consumers' needs. Because when one students feel home time is not enough to use computer to do their homeworkers at homes. When some students finish all lessons in schools and they need to catch public transportation tools to go home, in this catching public transportation time, they will be possible to hope to use one laptop computer to do their homeworks. So, one student who often feels time pressure to do whose homeworks, he will feel need to buy one laptop to carry it to anywhere, e.g. library, garden, school etc. different places. Then, he/she can do whom housework at any places in any time conveniently. Hence, it seems that their laptop computer products will be time pressure consumers' preference task tool.

In conclusion, the different factors influence consumer behaviors. Time pressure factor may be one main factor to influence consumers to choose to buy the kind of product or consume the kind of service in preference. So, when th consumer feels time presure to influence him/her to do preference choice to consume the kind of service of buy the kind of product. It is possible to occur to influence he/she does irrational economic choice decision. Hence, time pressure factor can being positive or negative both consumption emotion to some kinds of services or products . Hence, the increasing or decreasing number of consumers to some kinds of products or services, it has absolute relationship between of them. So, any product sellers or service providers can not neglect the importance of how time pressure factor influences consumer behavior in our nowadays society.

Time pressure impacts consumer behavioral effect

I shall indicate cases to explain that how time pressure environment factor impacts consumer behavior as well as what effects will be brought by time pressure consumer behavioral cause. Instead of above discussions concern how customer personal time pressure psychological factor influence, whether hoe time pressure environment factor will also influence consumer behavior. What are the difference between time pressure environment factor and time pressure consumer personal psychological factor? I shall explain as below:

Firstly, the impact of life satisfaction is caused by time pressure on consumers responses. Can effective advertising can impact of life satisfaction when the consumer feels need to buy the kind of product in any time pressure environment? Can effective advertising bring direct impact on sales when the consumer feels need to buy the kind of product in time pressure environment? Effective advertising may being advantages, includes customers feel easy to accept of price increases, favorable publicity, and reshaping market segmentation.

However, when the customer feels need life satisfaction in time pressure lif environment. The time pressure life environment ought impact on the consumer responses on advertising. Hence, when the consumer needs to live in the time pressure life environment. The over-commercialization of advertising ought impact the consumer chooses to buy the brand of product, when the seller has attractive advertising to bring purchase incentives to influence consumption desire to the time pressure environment influential consumer. For example, when the summer season will change to winter season, the ice cream consumers begins to feel weather will change to cold weather. Because many people feel more colf in the beginning. This is seasonable time pressure environment feeling, it may influence many ice-cream likers feel ice-cream may be possible shortage in hot weather or summer season, due to many ice-creams will be bought in summer weather to cause supermarkets in possible. So, if the brand ice-cream can make attractive advertisement to persuade ice-incre021 number will be reduced in the coming winter season beginning. So, it may influence many ice-cream likers choose to buy this brand's ice-cream in preference in summer. Because they feel fear none of any this brand's ice-creams can be sold in supermarkets in summer. Because they feel this brand's ice-cream , it's problem to let they can buy any different kinds of ice-cream taste to eat from any supermarkets in summer season. Hence, it explains why effective or attractive advertising may increase sale number, when consumers feel the brand's product number will be shortage or reduced from the seasonal time pressure external environment factor influence.

Secondly, I shall discuss what is the relationship between the effects of product popularity and time pressure on consumer responses? When a brand is popular to let many customers to familiarize in society. Does it increase time pressure to influence consumers choose in preference? Time pressure remaining to product popularity concerns how much sale number is raised to persuade consumers to choose to buy a preference for ecommerce online shopping. It seems to be one time pressure online sale environment. The effects of the ecommerce online shopping environment has relationship beteen pressure and product popularity on perceived risk and purchase intention.

In ecommerce online sale environment time pressure is operationized at the time remaining for consumers to sign up the online seller' website and property popularity is operationlized to the number of products already sold at the moment when consumers visit the web page. Hence, when on online consumer has intention to buy any products from internet. He/ she will attempt to type the product name, then he/she will find some webpages which can provide the different brands of product photos, their prices informations to let the consumer to compare whether which brand of product price is more reasonable, better quality , good product image from the web pages' advertisement information to let him/her to evaluate. Hence, any product web page will influence how every online custmer feeling is good or bad to the web page's any brands of products. If the consumer feel the web page has many high product popularity indicators, it may bring a high consumption desire to let the online cusomer to evaluate the web page all prodocts in order to compare which brand of product is the best to choose to buy in time webpage view pressure consumption environment. Otherwise, if the consumer feels the web page has high product popularity indicator , it may bring a less consumption desire to let the online consumer to evaluate any of the webpage products to choose to buy. So, online webpage advertising information will be one time pressure online ecommerce consumption environment.

I assume that online shopping consumers won't like to stay to view on any webpage long time. It is possible that they choose to click more web pages to hope to find more different familiar and unfamiliar both brands of products informations in order to make more accurate comparison and evaluation from more different kinds of brands of products in order to make the most accurate online shopping decision. Hence, any brands of products online webpage information will be one time pressure limited sale environment to consumers feel that they need to make the most accurate online purchase decision in short time. Moreover, it seems that if the brand of products which can be showed on the popular product webpage, the it will have much sale chance to let online purchasers familiarize in order to increase sale opportunity more easily.

Finally, I shall explain what is the meaning of external time pressure consumption environment is the long time queue waiting consumption environment. I shall explain how to achieve one simplistic queueing system to solve long time queue waiting problem to bring consumers' negative emotion influence to choose to consume the service or buy the product in preference.

For entertainment service example, e.g. queueing at the cinema counter to buy one ticket to watch the movie , or queueing at the music hall to buy one ticket to listen the music performance show activities. The audiences' ticket purchase aims to sit down in the cinema or music hall to enjoy to listen and see pretty music performance or watch the attractive movie comfortable within one to two hours entertainment time. If the movie or music performance show is attractive, the cinema or music hall will have many audiences accept to spend long time to queue to buy the ticket. However, if the cinema ot music hall needs audience consumers to queue long time to buy the ticket, e.g. one houe , even more than one houe queueing time to wait to buy the ticket to watch the movie or listen the music performance show. Then, the long time queue waiting problem will be possible to cause a lot audiences number to be reduced, because they feel that they need to spend much time pressure to queue to by the ticket to listen the music performance show or watch the movie.

However, of these unacceptable too long queue time audiences can have another/ other cinema(s), music hall(s) to buy the same price , even more low price of movie ticket or music performance show ticket in short time. Then, they must leave the present cinema queue and go to the another cinema or music hall to buy ticket to watch the same movie or listen the same music performance show. So, long time queue is one external time pressure environment to influence consumer's preference choice to the service provider, when they feel it has another service provider does not need them or these audiences need to spend same long time queue time to wait to buy the ticket in order to enjoy the service, e.g. listening music performance show, watching movie.

Hence, in a high time pressure queue situation where decision makers, e.g. audiences have less time than needed (or perceived needed). It is very likely that they feel the queue waiting time stress of copying with themselves queue waiting time maximum limitation. So, if the movie ticket purchase audience feels that he/she will need to spend more than half hour to queue and half hour is himself/herself the maximum acceptable queue time level. So, his/her queue long time pressur negative emotion feeling will influence him/her to leave the cinema to choose another cinema. He/she feels that ir does not need him/her to queue more than half hour in order to buy the ticket to watch the same movie in the another cinema, he/she can feel more comfortable to watch the movie. So, long time queue will influence some audiences choose aother service provider to replace it in possible short time, when they feel waiting in a queue is irritating, frustrating and hence costly.

What is a simplistic queueing system and how it can solve above queue problem. For a grocery store queueing counter case example, for one Apply brand computer shop example, the day's most busy queue time , there are about between fifty and hundred Apply brand potential computer buyers numbers every hour in the day. They need to queue to enquire the salespeople concern to any useful opinions to let them to know in order to make purchase decisions. But, the Apple brand computer shop lacks enough salespeople to answer their enquiries concern any computer purchase challenges. Every computer enquiry potential purchaser needs to spend at least half hour , even more time to queue to wait the salesperson to answer his/her enquiry in the counter queueing line. Hence, the feeling long time queue enquiry waiting consumers will feel time pressure to queue. Then, they will choose to leave the Apple brand computer shop's counter queue line. Consequently, the Apple brand computer will lose many potential computer buyers on the busy day.

The most simple solution is that it can increase the salespeople number in the most busy enquiry time every day. Hence, when every computer potential enquiry customer can contact every salesperson to listen whom opinion concerns his/her any computer enquiry issues in order to let he/

she feels that they every one can provide excellent sale service computer issues enquiry explanation performance to satisfy his/her enquiry need to let himself/herself to feel in the short enquiry time. Due to they do not need to spend long queue time to wait every salesperson's feedback or opinion to solve their enquiries in the computer shop. Because they do not feel presure to spend long time to queue to wait the computer shops's every salesperson's opinion. So, they will raise satisfactory feeling to thie Apple computer shop's every salesperson individual sale enquiry service performance.

Consequently, the day's computer sale number will be possible to raise after the salespeople can spend much time to solve their enquiries effectively and efficiently.

● The reasons cause consumers feel
time pressure

What factors can cause consumers feel time pressure to but the product in the personal time limited dominated consumption environment? It is one interesting question: Why does the consumer feel time pressure to make short time purchase decision making? I shall indicate some cases to explain this possibility as below:

First, I shall indicate household purchaser time pressure consumption behavior. Consumer house buyer behavior, some house buyer will feel personal time pressure to choose the different houses to make house purchase decision in short time. For example, if the house developer has a 30% discount house price to sell only in the short three months. So, after this three months, all house purchaser will need to pay the original house price. If the house developer's houses prices are between US doller one million to two million every house. For one million house price after 30% discount , the house buyer only needs to pay seventy million. For two million house price after 30 % discount, the house buyer only needs to pay one hundred and fourty million. So, expensive product's financing factor will influence the buyer's consumption time pressure, such as the house discount price case, due to the house developer's houses prices are very expensive. However, if any house buyers can make decisin to buy its houses in three months. Then, they can pay les 30% of the houses prices. Such as the original price one million house, the house buyer can pay less thirty million amount or the original price two million houses prices. The house buyer can pay less sixty million amount. So, the large discount financing amount may be attractive purchase method to influence many house buyers feel time pressure to decide whether they ought choose to buy the property developer's houses in these three months. It is one short term cheap house financing price to let many house buyers feel time pressure to make house purchase decision from this house developer in these three months . Hence, short term high discount price to expensive product financing factor will influence consumers feel it is right time to make pressure consumption decision.

Hence, such as this three months house discount price case, when the property buyer gain this property developer's knowledge of three months house discount price message. This sudden three months house discount price message will be one attractive knowledge of factor to impact the potential property buyers' house purchase desires to be raised in three months time pressure house purchase consumption environment. So, it is one feeling sudden time pressure consumption desire good example for this three monts large discount attractive houes price to influence house buyers to make house purchase decision from the house developer in these three months. Consequently, house developer will have possible to raise the large house sale number , if this 30 % house discount price can let many property buyers feel it is one worth purchase price in these three months. So, they will consider that they can not pay less 30% discount price to buy this house developer's any houses after three months. So they need to make house purchase decision in these three months short term time pressure house consumption market for this property developer.

So, this time pressure financing advantage will only bring benefit to this property developer, this time pressure financing advantage won't bring benefit to other property developers, because all property buyers feel need to make property purchase decision in these three months suddenly, due to this property developer can provide a special 30 discount price to any property final decision making to choose to buy its houses in these three months temporary short time. It seems that three months short time can cause final house purchase choice time pressure to any potential property buyers. They expect to gain high discount price to buy any expensive houses. So, these expenaive house potential buyers will feel need to make final expensive house purchase decision to choose to buy this property developer's expensive houses in these final three months perios. So, time pressure can occur in any short period, when the seller can provide any special sale promotion to persuade consumers to feel need to make sudden time pressure that purchase decision is they hope to earn special sale promotion consumption in the short limited sale perios for the seller.

Hence, consumer personal time pressure feeling, it can be predictive to any time occurrence pychological consumption, feeling, such as the property developer's sudden high per cent discount price to expensive house less dinancing burden factor to influence the expensive house buyers feel that whether they ought do choice house purchase decision in these short term three months , because the house developer's unpredictive and sudden attractive expensive houses reducing prices strategy. So, this property developer's short term three months high house discount price time pressure consumption strategy may persuade or attract , even encourage many potential expensive house buyers choose to spend lesser amount to buy this property developer's discount houses, either is paid by house mortgage bank loan lending payment method or installment payment method or on-time all payment method. So, the different house payment choice buyers will be influenced to make immediate property purchase decision in these three months time pressure period from this property developer's expensive discounted house number influence.

However, in this house market time pressure consumption environment, the property developer's expensive house supply number may also have influential effort to excite the expensive house buyers' house purchase consumption desires, for example, if the other expensive house property developers' between US one million and US two million of every property price's these houses in the country's property marker totel suppy number is one thousand property unit number. The potential property buyers , they plan to buy these amounts of expensive houses , the property needers estimate three thousand buyers number at least. Hence, it seems that these expensive house buyers' demand id more than three times to expensive property supply number.

Moreover, the other property developer's expensive property developers ' expensive house prices have no any discount in this three months periods, and some property developers' expensive house prices tend to increase 1 to 10 per cent in these three months period. Hence if the property developer can supply at least three thousand property units number between US one million and US two million sale price and all of these expensive houses are reduced 30 per cetnt discount to sell in these three months .

Consequently, it is possible to persuade all estimated three thousand expensive house potential buyers choose to buy this property developer's houses in these three months in possible. So, it explain that why this property developer's expensive discounted house supply number will influence these property buyers' preference choice. If this property developer has only one thousand expensive houses to be supplied by discounted 30% sale price. Then, it will cause shortage of expensive houses to satisfy these three thousand expensive house buyer estimated number in the country in three month discount sale promotion period.

Consequently, this property developer will lose two thousand these prices of expensive house potential buyers number in all these three months discounted sala period . I assume that all these three thousand expensive house property buyers will be influenced to make choice to buy its all dicounted expensive houses in these three month time pressure discounted sale period. So, it needs to do data gather concerns how many of thee expensive house potential house buyers number in its country in order to avoid discounted expensive houses supply number to cause shortage supply challenges and bring these expensive house potential buyers lose number in these three months period.

In conclusion, it explains why that supply number will influence this property developer's sale number in these three months sale period. Consequently, time pressure sale strategy ans supply number has close relationship to influence the seller's sale number in the time pressure sale period.

Secondly, I shall discuss how does environment time pressure factor influences consumer behavior? Does time pressure influence consumer donating behavior? I assume that external environment time pressure factor can influence consumer changes whom original purchase decision making. What circumstance's time can influence consumer individual to feel time pressure to consume. For example, when the consumer expects have one hour to choose whether which brand of product to buy among the different kinds of products. The circumstance is changed suddenly. It influences the consumers feel that they has only 10 minutes to make the final purchse decision.

Why does the consumer feel enough brand of product? What external circumstance factors influence he/she feels only 10 minutes time to make the final purchase decision suddenly? For travel fair time limited external environment influential pressure travelling consumption case example, the international travel fair can indicate that time limited pressure has positive significant influence on traveller perceived value and purchase intention in short time. In addition, perceived value is served as a mediating factor between the relationship of time limited pressure and feeling travelling entertainment purchase intention to the travel fair visitors. It has a beneficial reference for planning a travelling show or fair marketing strategy.

One attractive travelling fair/show can promote the country's different attractive travelling destinations to let the travellinf show's visitors to know. It can particularly influence the visitors' long time travelling planning , it can be shorten be short time travelling planning, e.g. after one year's travelling planning can be influenced to make immediate focused on choosing the country's travelling decision if he/she feels the country has more attractive travelling destinations, he/she prefers to go to travel in short time, e.g. within 6 months . So, when the travelling exhibition fair/show can provide the country's beautiful scene photos to let the visitors to view. Then, it will bring effective time pressure feeling to let some travelling visitos feel travelling needs immediately in the travelling exhibition show/fair . This travelling exhibition show/fair can bring the time limited pressure benefit. It is as an external environment factor that can influence the travelling visitors' travelling desires to be raised , when they can view many benefitical scene photos of the country' different undiscovered travelling destination . Then, it can increase their travelling desires to the country in possible.

I shall explain why travelling exhibition show/fair can play an important role in travelling consumer perceived quality and travelling country destination choice decision making to influence travelling visitors feel time limited pressure. However, perceived value has been show to be a value has been shown to be a value of perceived quality and perceived sacrifice to cause travelling visitors feel more interesting to choose to travel the country when they can view the attractive beautiful scence photos in the travelling exhibition show/fair.

A successful travelling exhibition show/fair can bring time limited process increases , the travelling visitors pay more attention to key travelling destination features and positive travelling information from the scene photos and travelling destinations introduction. So , the country's attractive travelling destinations scene photos and clear travelling introduction to different destinations information will be important message to let the different countries' travelling visitors to know when they spend a limited time to enter the travelling exhibition show/fair to view the different scene photos . If the travelling visitor feel very satisfied to the country's travelling exhibition show/fair. Then, this travelling exhibition excite whom travelling interest to choose to go to the country to travell in short time, when the travelling visitors are influenced to feel the country has many beautiful destinations where they feel have travelling interest in the limited time pressure travelling exhibition show/fair environment. If the travelling exhibition show/fair needs they to pay enter fee and it has only two hours or less time to premit to stay in the travelling exhibition show/fair.

Hence, if the time pressure limited travelling exhibition show/fair can let the travelling visitors feel attractive and enjoyable view feeling when they look every the country's any scene beautiful photos and indication how to the different travelling destinations and explains why the country's travelling places are value travelling destinations to let the exhibition visitors to know, when they do not know or discover these any one of value travelling places in the country before. Then, this limited time staying travelling exhibition show/fair will bring positive time pressure to influence some travelling visitors feel interesting to visit the country's inknown or undiscovery travelling destinations in short time. So, all attractive travelling exhibition shows/fairs are one external environment time limited positive pressure factor to excite some travelling visitors' travelling desires in short time in possible.

Instead of travelling exhibition show/fair can bring external environment positive limited time positive pressure to excite travelling visitors' travelling consumption desires, the another external environment positive limited time positive pressure case is that mobile coupons of limited mobile phone sale number or discount mobile phone call payment plan in short time case. How and why mobile coupons can excite any mobile consumption and/ or mobile phone call user choice to the mobile phone sale company or mobile phone call service provider.

An effective mobile plane useful limited time beneficial purchase strategy can encourage some mobile phone consumers to choose to use the brand mobile useful phone call service plan immediately. if the mobile phone call service plan is attractive to the mobile phone call consumer . For example, dynamic discounts strategies are used by marketers to send scaraity message which lead to higher consumers' mobile phone purchase intention. An utility increasing discount straregy provides mobile phone call users with an increasing discount over time (e.g. 30% discount for in-store consumption for 30 minutes, after which the discount increases to 40 % , an utility discount strategy provides the same discounts for mobile phone call users over a specific promotional period (e.g. 40% discount from 9AM to 5 PM) phone call using time. An utility decreasing discount strategy offers mobile phone call users with a decreasing discount over time (e.g. 40% discount for in -store consumption for 10 minutes, after which the discount decreases to 30%).

However, these three different discount strategies for bargaining have different impacts on outcomes. However, they have same influences to lead mobile phone call users feel time pressure to do choose whether this mobile phone call using plan is suitable. If the mobile phone call user feels this mobile phone call using plan is suitable to use, then this mobil coupon promotion strategy can influence mobile phone user feels limited time pressure to persuade him/her to choose to use its mobile phone call service under different time limitation, quantity limitation and discount strategies on the mobile phone user's mobile phone call plan using intention.

Furthermore, I hypothesize that the brand of mobile phone quantity, limited scarcity message that gives a perception that the brand of any kinds of mobile phones are limited for purchase, it will have a positive impact on mobilt phone consumers' perceived value of mobile products, leading to a greater tendancy to make mobile phone purchase decision immediately. Hence, mobile coupon is one type of price-incentive promotion. In various price incentives, discount strategy is a mode of price negotiation between the mobile product conumer and the merchant, such as the mobile phone seller , mobile phone call user and mobile phone call service provider.

However, mobile coupons offer discount under a time constraint to induce perceived scarcity. Scarce commodities are more attractive than those with plenty inventory due to the speciality and uniqueness of the former perceived by the consumer. However, scarcity has both forms. They incluce quantity scaracity can let consumers feel need to buy the product in short time. Otherwise, due to stock shortage or low inventory to influence they can not brought the kind of product. Time scarcity means products are for sale only for a designated

CHAPTER FIVE

May time dominate consumption final purchase decision making

Whether can time limited pressure dominate consumer individual to make more rational purchase decision? Can the consumer make more rational decision , when he/she has enough time to make final purchase decision? I shall explain why and how the consumer can make more rational decision when he/she has enough time as well as I shall explain that without time pressure environment. It may dominate consumers to make more rational or more accurate decision making.

I assume that it is the final time limited pressure day to need the consumer to spend more nervous do time final purchase decision among the different kinds of similar products choices, e.g. air conditions . If the consumer decides that the day is the final purchase decisin to choose to buy one air conditin among these different brands of similar air conditions in the super store. So, if on the that day, he/she can not make any final decisin to choose which brand of air condition to buy on that final consumption day in the super store when the super store visitor sees the final air condition consumption day advertisement in this year in this super store . Then, he/she won't buy any air condition again if he/she can not buy on that day in this super store.

The another time dominates immediate purchase behavior is that I assume that one common air condition can not be bought in short time later if all air condition consumers can not make decision to buy any air condition in this super store. So, his/her personal time limited pressure can dominate whose final or condition purchase decision in this super store on that day. If the store has many different brands of air conditions to lead him/her to spend long time to compare which is th best worth to buy in this super store. Then, it will let him/her to feel difficult to make the air condition final purchase decision in the store on that day. Otherwise, if the super store has less different brands of air conditions to need him/her to spend less time to compare which is the best worth to buy in the store. Then, he/she may make the final air conditin purchase decision making more easily on that day.

So, the final air condition purchase day of the super store, the super store's air condition final day's time can dominate the air condition buyer to make air condition purchase decision immediately. Due to he/she feels that all of thesc day brands air conditions can not bought from this super store after that day. So, he/she needs to make the air condition purchase decision making in this super store on that final air condition purchase day in this year. Because it is the final air condition purchase day in this super store of all sir conditions products. If he/she can not make the choice to buy any one brand of air condition in this store. Then, it is possible that he/she will lose this store's final cheap price air condition purchase benefits. However, if this super store has too many brands of air conditions need him/her to choose. It will cause him/her to spend more time to choose. Consequently, it will cause he/she feels difficult to compare which brand of air condition is the best and he / she does not choose to buy any one in this super store. Hence, this super store ought have less number different brands of air conditions to let every air condition consumer to choose in order to let they can make final air condition purcahse decision on this air condition cheap price purchase final day. So, less different number brands of air conditions will dominate the consumers to spend less time to make purchase decision immediately and easily on that final sale day in this super store. Hence, it seems that the super store's final air conditions sold day time will dominate many air condition visitors to make purchase decision when they visit this super store in summer season on that day in this super store. Because all this super store's air condition consumers do not expect that they can not buy the best quality of air conditin in this super store final sold day , due to air condition stocks number shorten challenge is not supplied enough on that final cheap purchase day in this super store. Consequently, that time pressure will increase to influence them to make the final air condition purchase decision in the final sold day' s short time, before this super store closing time on that day. Their time pressure feeling comes from the super store 's air condition number shortage supply in possibility. It will dominate them to make the final air condition purchase decision in this super store in short time.

The anothe time dominates immediate purchase behavior case is that I assume that one common picture painter(actor), he finds one architect to help him to build one house. The architect only needs to folloe his house picture to build one house. The common picture painter tells him that he will give him building expenditure and building profit after he helps him to build the house profit after he helps him to build the house successfully. After six months, the architect made one decision, he did not demand the famous picture painter paid him for the building service fee. But, he needed him give the house picture to him to replace the building service fee. Because the picture painter feels that he didn't need to pay the building service fee to him to buy the architect's building service in these six months building time. Hence, he accepted his offer to give his common house picture to the architect for his reward.

I assume that this six months time dominate the architect to make the final building service fee decision either acceptance the common picture painter customer's building service fee or acceptance his common house picture replaces the building service fee. However, the architect believes that this common house picture can have higher selling price to compare his building service fee income. Consequently, I assume that his evaluation is right, this house picture selling price is more than three times to compare his past six months's building service income. So, it proved that his choice is right, because he could earn more than three times of his building service income after he decided to accept the common picture painter's this house picture to attempt to sell it in the picture auction market. It seems that this six months long house building time can dominate these both buyer and seller's purchase and selling behaviors, such as this picture painter and this architect. When the architect has this six months enough time to let the picture painter to change his building service offer decision from building service fee payment to his common house picture offer exchange. This architect can achieve his intention to let him to accept his free house picture sold product exchange offer more easily. Otherwise, if the architect can not need six months to build this house, he only needs three months or less time to build this house, then it is possible that the picture painter won't accept his this house picture offer to replace his building service fee easily. If he considers that whether his this house picture's selling price has possible to sell higher price to compare this building service fee for this house picture.

He will choose to sell this house picture himself. Hence, due to the picture painter can not sell this house picture in this past six months. So, in this six months period, the house painter can not sell this house picture in picture auction market. This six months period can dominate his low market worth selling feeling to this house picture as well as it can influence him to make this house picture exchange decision to replace his house service fee.

The picture painter will ask himself, ought the house picture painter need to wait how long time to sell this picture in auction market, because he does not know whether the architect needs how long time to build this house? So, this house building time can dominate the picture painter's acceptance of the architect's this free house picture product exchange offer, which is easier acceptance or difficult acceptance . In this six month' house building period between the architect service provider and the picture painter house buyer. Hence,the house building time can dominate the house building provider and the picture painter's house building buyer both's house picture free exchange purchase change behavioral choice between of them influentially.

The another time dominates consumption behavior case is that time rich or time poor factor, e.g. one fast food famous restaurant , its success is not only due to its fast food good taste factor, its restaurant location whether is close to the time poor people's offices, it is one main factor. Because this fast food famous restaurant only choose to build its restaurants to close to offices in any large cities in different countries. Hence, the franchisees need to pay expensive franchise loyalty income to buy its franchise in order to it can supply fast foods to the franchisees to sell, but they also need to pay expensive rent to this fast food franchiser, due to their fast food restaurant locations has been chose to locate in the main cities in different countries from the fast food famous restaurant's location decision. Hence, whether long or short time fast restaurant rent period to the franchisees , which can dominate the fast food restaurants's royalty and rent income. For example, if one fast food franchisee only sign one year contract to buy the fast food franchisor's loyalty to help it to sell its fast foods only one year, because it does not ensure how many fast food consumers will choose to buy these fast foods to eat, due to its price is decided by the fast food franchisor. If the cities have other fast food restaurants to let them to choose, they may find other fast food restaurants to replace it to eat fast foods very easily. If this fast good restaurant is not the most famous and it operates only short time. So, it can not earn more fast food franchisees' confidence to accept to pay long time rent to operate its fast food restaurants in cities and pay long time royalty fee to it. Otherwise, if the fast food restaurant had operated its restaurant for a long time period to raise its fast food loyalty's to let many different countries' fast food eaters to familiarize or acknowledg its fast food brand in popular. So, long fast food opersation time can confirm that it has many fast food eaters, they prefer to choose to eat its fast foods. It can increase the franchisees' confidence to choose to rent its fast food restaurants and pay royalty to it in preference. Hence, the fast food franchisor's restaurant operation time whether it is long or short time, this franchisor's fast food restaurant operating time pressure factor will dominate the fast food franchisees' choices to decide to pay how long rent sand franchise royalty income to rent its restaurant to do the franchisee's fast food business in the cities locations in different countries. So, it seems that the fast food franchisor's business operation time can dominate the frahchisees' choice.

In special , in fast food industry, time rich and time poor consumers behavior will dominate their fast food choices. Time rich people feel they have enough or too much time when time poor people feel time is a major constraint in their daily life. The explansion of the fast food business, and the increase eatting of fast food are indicators of this trend. At the same time, shorter working hours increased wealth and less pressure on domestic rountines have opened up new segments of leisure consumption. But, " free time" in certain areas has not for many people, lead to an increases feeling of time richness.

So, it explains that why many fast food consumers who feel not enough time to work daily. They are time poor working people usually. So, instead of fast food taste factor influences consumer number. The people who feel time rich or poor, e.g. employmet rich or poor lunch time to the employee, it will dominate the employee chooses to go to fast food restaurant in preference. So, the fast food restaurant can supply rich time to let them to eat lunch in short time, if the employee has less time to eat lunch or more tasks need hime to do on that day afternoon. Hence, feeling time rich or poor to the people factor, which will dominate some consumers' choices to some kinds of businesses, such as fast food industry, or for public transportation tool choice case example, one time poor passenger feels need to go to the destination in short time. The time poor passenger will prefer to choose taxi in preference, then it is possible train or underground train, next it is tram, fainally, it is bus or ferry public transportion tool choices. Otherwise, for one time rich passenger, he has more time to go to the destinaton. The time rich passenger will prefer to choose the cheap public transportation tool , such as bus, ferry, underground train, ferry, train. The final choice is taxi. So, passenger's time pressure will influence whose public transportation tool choice.

● Time pressure dominiates consumer psychological factor

What are the factors of time pressure dominate consumer purchcase psychological behaviors? How any why do this time pressure psychological factors dominate consumer behaviors? It is possible that time pressure can dominate consumer mind and behavior either choose to buy the product/consume the service or not buy the product/consume the service. Every consumer's final purchase decision, he/she is influenced how to make by himself/herself personal psychological limited time pressure . It means that he/she will have one time maximum standard to demand himself/herself to make the final purchase decision in whose individual psychological time standard (the consumer's individual psychological limited consumption time). So, it seems that ever consumer's final decision how he/she chooses to buy the product or consume the service, his/her consumption behavior will be dominated by whose psychological time limited consumption pressure.

So, time pressure issue seems evolutionary psychology, it looks at how consumer behavior has beed affected by psychological adjustments during time pressure evoluation. It seeks to identify which consumer psychological traits are evolved through adaptations, e.g. time pressure consumption adaptations to choose the final purchase decision in the final time limited consumption pressure environment, e.g. the consumer expects this day is the final day to choose to buy what kinds of the product. If he/she can't make final purchase decisin on the day, he/she will choose to buy the kind of product later, even he/she does not choose to buy the kind of product in the first or again, that is the products of natural selection, or the supermaket visitor case, he expects to choose which kind of food to eat within final 15 minutes, if he/she can't make the final decision to buy what kind of food to eat within final 15 minutes in this supermarket , or the restaurant eatting consumer case, he is queueing to wait to enter the restaurant to eat. He/she expects the final queue waiting time is 15 minutes maximum. If after this 15 minutes, he/she can not be permited to enter this restaurant, then he/she will choose to leave this restaurant and he/she will find another restaurant to replace it. So, it seems that any consumer will have himself/

herself consumption limited stardard time to decide whether he/she ought choose to buy any products or consume any services in any consumption environment.

Hence, the cause of consumption time pressure dominates consumer behavior, it is based on these hypothesis: Every consumer has demand characteristic and time pressure can dominate how he/she make final decision to buy or not buy any product or consume any service as well as any consumer needs have time pressure consumption demand because he/she does not expect to epend more time to choose what kinds of products to buy or what kinds of services to consume. He/she expects to make purchase or consumption final decision in short time.

IN fact, consumers will be encoded to influence how they make final purchase decision. There are three main ways in which product information can be encoded. They include: Visual (product picture) ; for example, the conumer stores the memory by visualizing it as on product image. Aconstic (sound); here the consumer stores the information as a sound , this explains why some consumers sometimes get the brand name(words) that sound the same mixed up when they try to remember them. Semantic (meaning); here the object is stored in terms of what it means rather than as an image or sound, e.g. when the brand of toys can let many children feel fun to play. Then, when many parents feel familiar to the toy brand, they must remember this toy brand company is selling any kinds of toys to let children to play. So, famous brand can let consumers familiarize what products that it is selling. Such as the toy brand company can let parents feel its toys are fun to let their children to play. All these sensory information can dominate consumers make final choice purchase behavior to buy its product or consume its service in preference in any time limited pressure environment, if the brand can give positive information memory to let many customers to remember.

So, it seems that consumers are dominated to choose which kinds of products to buy or which kinds of services to consume by positive or negative emotion, time pressure in any consumption environment immediately. It is one time pressure consumption environment theory factor, it can influence consumer behavior is changed in any consumption environment time. Consequently, it explains that why time pressure can dominate consumer behaviors in possible. Also, any product seller or service provider needs to consider how to manage consumption time process to be longer to cause its consumers doe not choose to buy its product or consume its service consequently.

Methods avoid consumers
feel time pressure

In business society, it seems that any consumers will feel time pressure to cause their purchase decision making process changes in any consumption suitations, when they feel time pressure either by themselves or third parties influence, e.g. not buying any thing, not consuming any service, irrational making consumption final decision etc. consumption behaviors. How to reduce their time pressure to avoid they do above consumption behaviors. I shall indicate some consumption suitations to explain how to avoid their reducing consumption , due to time pressure factor influences as below:

Firstly, I shall indicate supermarket consumption environment example. In general, supermarket visitors will expect to spend less time to visit any supermarkets to make choice to biy any foods. They will stay short time when they expect to buy less foods, even, they will stay more short time when they expect to buy more less foods in any supermarkets. So, any supermarkets will need to calculate their clients' limited time pressure how to influence their foods consumption number. If the supermarket visitor expects to spend maximum 20 minutes to buy any foods in the supermarket. Then, he may choose some different kinds of foods to buy, e.g. icecream, fruit, bread, jam, fish etc. different kinds of foods, Otherwise, if the another supermarket visot expects to spend maximum 10 minutes to buy any foods in the supermarket. Then, he may choose less different kinds of foods to compare the first one, e.g. fish, jam, icecream only or bread, fruit , jam only. So, the second one supermarket visitor will buy less different kinds of foods, because he expects to spend 10 minutes maximum , his shopping spending time is less 10 minutes to compare the first one supermarket visitor. Because different supermarket visitor personal time pressure will limit him/her to choose more or less different kinds of foods to buy. However, time pressure will not influence every kind of foods number because every kind of food purchase number will not be influenced to buy more or less , due to the supermarket visitor personal time pressure variable factor influences his/her foods purchase number. Otherwise, the different kinds of food choice will be influenced to choose to either buy or not buy , due to every supermarket visitor personal time pressure is different.

Hence, supermarkets can focus on how to avoid any kinds of food purchase choice loses , due to supermarket consumer personal time pressure influences. In fact, in supermarket every shelf, it usually has many different brands of every kind of foods to let supermarket visitors to choose to buy. For example,the kind of jam food number has many brands are placed on shelf to let them to choose, e.g. there are more than 10 different brands of jam food are placed on one shelf. It will bring one choice problem. IF one supermarket visitor expects to choose one brand of jam within 5 minute, then he finds the shelf has more than 10 different brands of jam are placed on the shelf. Then he will feel time pressure to cause difficulty to choose the best brand of jam to buy from these 10 brands of jam. It will bring the negative emotion if he feels that all of these 10 brands of jam taste and price has no more difference. Consequently, these 10 brands of jam choice will cause he can not make the final jam purchase decision within this 5 minutes individual time limited. Anyway, if there are only 5 brands of jam are placed on this shelf, then the 5 minutes time limited consumer will has less brands of jam choices, it will influence him to do more easy choice to buy one kind of brand jam food from the shelf. It is one limited time pressure of psychological choice factor to influence any consumers feel to do any brand of food choice more easy in short time. Hence, I recommend supermarket shelf ought place every kind of food brand maximum to 5 brands , it is the best food brand number to every supermarket's shelves to let any consumers to choose different kinds of foods to make the easy food choice way in supermarket food market.

So, in super store market, it is similar to supermaket market. Super stores' main products are cloths, shoes, bags, stationarys, electronic products, e.g. fans, air conditions, televisons, radios, warmers, washing machines, dry machines, computers etc. However, super store visitors will like to spend more time to stay in any super stores, due to they feel to need more time to make purchase decision in order to make the most right choice to buy these any products. They usually expect to stay half hour , even one hour or more time in super stores. Their time pressures are depended on whether what kinds of products that they expect to buy in the super store. For example, if the super store visitor expects to buy one laptop computer. He will expect to make purchase choice decision within half hour, even more time. Otherwise, if the super store visitor expects to buy stationery, e.g. pen and rubber and pencil, he will expect to make purchase choice decision within 10 minutes. So, when the super store visitor expects to buy the product is more expensive, then his time pressure time will be longer than the super store visior expects to buy the product is cheap, such as stationery and laptop two kinds of products.

However , due to super store 's expensive and cheap product consumers whose time pressures are different. So, brands choice number will have much different between them. For laptop example, due to superstore visitors can accept to spend longer time to make laptop purchase choice. So, one shelf can place 5 to 10 different brands of laptops , another shelf can place 5 to 10 different brands of laptops to let them to choose. Otherwise, for stationery example, due to superstore visitors can not accept to spend longer time to make stationery purchase choice. so, one shelf can place less than 5 brands of pens, the another shelf can place less than 5 brands of pencils or another shelf can place less than 5 brands of rubbers , another shelf can place less than 5 brands of rulers to let them to make purchase choice in short time.

Secondly, for restaurant eaters example, when one restaurant has many eaters choose to enter this restaurant to eat its food, then it only chooses to let some eaters to enquire ticket number to queue to wait. Of course, some eaters will not like to wait too long time, so they will leave the queue to choose another restaurant to replace it in possible. For example, in afternoon eating time, these are two busy eaters, the student feels hurry to go to school or the working person feels hurry to go to office after lunch, although the restaurant service staff had given him one ticket to let them to queue to wait. However, their expected queue waiting time is within 15 maximum, but there are many eaters are queuing and their ticket numbers are small numbers. So, they feel that they must not enter this restaurant within 15 minutes themselves limited queue time. Consequently, their late entering this restaurant after 15 minutes issue will influence that they will choose another restaurant in possible. So, the restaurant long time queue will cause some eaters choose another restaurant in busy time. I recommend that the restaurant can limit every eater's eatting time, e.g. it calculate every eater's restaurant entering time and it limits every must leave the restaurant within half hour in busy eatting time. It can post notice to let them to know in the front door, e.g. Every eater needs to leave our restaurant within half hour, otherwise, you will need to bring your food to leave please. So, every eater know that they need to eat all food within half hour, otherwise, they need to bring their food to leave this restaurant. Then, this restaurant can increase more seats to let many queue waiting eaters , they do not queue to spend long time to wait to enter this restaurant. Consequently, many queue waiting eaters will choose to enter this restaurant, due to their queue waiting times are not exceed their time pressure limited time.

The final case is cinema queue . In general, any cinemas will have many audiences need to wait to buy tickets to watch movies. However, if the cinema has many audiences , they need to spend one hour, or two hours , even more than two hours to queue to wait to buy the ticket to watch any movies in the cinema. If some audiences' expected queue waiting times are within one hour. So, if these audiences' expected queue waiting timesa are more than one hour. Then, they will choose to leave this cinema and choose other cinemas to replace it in possible. How to avoid these time pressure audiences losing number increases in cinema busy time? I recommend that this cinema ought increase ticket purchase counter service staffs number , e.g. opening more three to five ticket purchase counters number in order to let these one hour time queue time waiting audiences can purchase ticket to watch their movies within one hour. So, opening urgent ticket purcahse service counters number issue is depended on whether there are how many audiences are waiting to buy ticket in the cinema in the time. However, it is only one best way to avoid the cinema audiences number loses in cinema busy time.

CHAPTER SIX

Time press how influences video playing game consumer purchase behavior

I shall explain that why it has relationship between the video game student consumer individual learning time and the working people individual working time both can influence video game playing consumer individual video game choice behavior. I shall assume that the different kinds of video game content difficult or easy win competition and entertainment spending on playing time factor will have more influence how the student or working person individual choice of what kind of video game purchase. Otherwisem evey video game price and brand and video game entertainment design content will have less inflience to every video game consumer individual purchase choice.

Why do the every video game's learning playing time and the playing time is spent to satisfy the feeling of winning game both factors will be the main factors to influence the feeling busy learning student or feeling rest working personal target video game playing consumer individual kind of which video game software purchase choice? Why do feeling busy learning students or feeling rest working people will be prefer to choose to buy the kinds of need spending little time to learn to play to achieve the easy winning of the video game content aim in short time?

Nowadays, the different brands of video game products have different prices, various entertainment design contents and the easy or difficult win content feeling to be promoted to sell to satisfy the students or working people video game players' entertainment needs. However, time pressure will be one important factor to influence students of working peoples' video games choices. I shall explain that the time pressure factor how will influence the feeling busy learning or feeling rest working video game players or video game content software consumers to choose to buy the kinds of video games softwares which can let them to feel to spend little playing and learning time and they can feel easy to win the the video game competition in short time preference in this electronic enterainment video game industry.

Nowadays, video game target customers, they are young students and adult working people in common. When , the student does not need to go to school and he/she stays at home, he /she will like to play video game after he/she finishs to learn just a moment usually or the adult working person finishs jobs on the day, after he/she ate dinner, he/she will also like to play video game at home. So , video game can be one kind of entertainment product to let they feel enjoy to play when they re staying at homes.

Video game can be one kind of entetainment culture or entertainment behavior at home to them in popular. A player's ability to perform within a game entertainment is important, and players tend to knowledgeable about their achievements and failures within any game world. So, when one student hopes toget pass grade in school examination. He will choose to spend little time to attempt to win the video game content competition in short time because it can let him to feel that may increase his confidence to pass the grade in the school examination later in possible when he ensures that he had won the video game content competition. He believes that he can be trained to raise whose judgement and mind and analysis abilitiy in his playing visdo game proceed. Instead of playing video game can increase student learning confidence, it can also increase the working people's confidence, when the working person hopes to be promoted or increased salary later from his supervisor's appreciation. He will attempt to spend little time to win the kind of video game content competition in short time. He will have more condifent to achieve to raise his working performance to let his supervisor appreciation if he can learn how to win the kind of video game competition in short time.

It seems that whether the player needs to spend how much time to learn how to win any kind of video content game competitin , this " spending learning time of winning any video content game competition in time pressure playing environment feeling factor will influence the student or working person 's video game content purchase choice. If the video game design is more complex or difficult to let the player to feel to learn to win the game competition as well as it also needs them to spend more long time to learn to play and win the kind of video content game competition. Then, it has possible to influence the hard learning students or hard working people video game consumers, they do not choose to buy any kinds of need spending long learning and playing time to win the kinds of video content game competitive software products. So, it seems that the spend how much playing and learning time to win the video game content competition factor will bring time pressure to let the hard working people or hard learning student video game consumers choose to buy the video content game software products are easy to learn to play in preference because they expect to pass grade or appreciate easy, if they feel that they can learn how to win the video game content competition in short time as well as they do not spend much playing time to win the kind of video game content competition and they will reduce their learning time at homes.

I shall explain why price won't be the main factor to influence video game players' purchase choices in preference. Some video game software sellers feel reduced sale price can attract many video game buyers' choice in preference. It is one wrong mind, due to video game software price is not too much high, it is one kind popular cheap entertainment software product. So , the kinds of similar entertainment content design video game products , their sale price difference between the kind of most expensive , the highest price video game software and the kind of the cheapest , the lowest price video game software won't be difference very much. Their price difference level may be US 410 to US\$50 or even less than US\$50 level. So,, one video fame entertainment player won't feel that the kind of similar content design of video game software's higher price which will influence he chooses to buy another cheaper similar of kind video game content design software product to replace to the prior higher price one. Because their price difference are not too much or video game software entertainment product is not on kind of expensive product to let them to feel. So, it seems what video game software price won't influence the video game players' prior one of preference choice, it is not easy to be replaced from later cheaper one, when the video game player feels like to play the kind of high price of video game content software before.

Can the video game content influence player individual purchase motivation in preference? In fact, there are many different kinds of video game contents to let players to choose. This free-to -play busines model that has rapidly speed to achieve games services to general . So, some students or working people players can free download some kinds of video game softwares to play from online channel. It will be attractive to the no paid video game players. Hence, free download video game content will influence the paid video game players' purchase decisions for in -game content are not only affected by people's existing general attitudes, consumption values, and movitations , but also by the design decisions and the needs built into the game by the developers. Because the paid video game players won't like to buy the similar content video games, which can be free download to play from online or internet channel. They will feel infair or not worth or loss if they choose to pay to buy the similar video game content entertainment software, after they discovered that they may be free download this kind of similar video game content to play from internet.

It will bring this question: Why will time pressure influence video game player chooses to download free video game to play in preference? When one student feels that he has no enough time to study, he won't choose to fo to any video game shops to do video game software comparative behavior to compare which one's price is lower, game playing content is more attractive, brand is familar in order to make final purchase decision in preference. If he discovered that there has one kind of video game content, which can be free download to play from internet or online channel . So, when the student feels that he needs have much time to study on the day. Hw will choose to attempt to find some kind of video game contents from computer tool which has the attractive entertainment content , it can let he to feel enjoy to play and it is free download from mobile or computer. Then, he won't choose to spend unpredictive time to visit any video game shops to make purchase decision on that day. So, time pressure will be one factor to influence some video game software consumers to feel whether they ought either visit any video game shops to make purchase choice or download some free video game contents at homes for the feeling no enought learning time student players. Even time pressure will also influence adult working people video game players, when the working person feels tries after his full day busy working on that day. Then, he will want to stay at home to rest . Although, he expects to visit any video game shops to choose which video game software product(s) to buy on that day, but when he discovered taht there are some video game contents which ar attractive to influence him to do free download behavior from internet at home. Also, he feels very tried and he will choose to stay at home on that day. If he can find some free video game contents are attractve to influence he chooses to do free download video game contents behavior and replace visiting video game stores behavior on that day. So, free download video game content entertainment activity will be one attractive promotin video game software method to assist the video game sellers' new video game products to let many feeling time pressure learning or working video game players to know from internet channel.

Consequently, online free entertainment video game content download playing choice will influence many video game shops will lose many feeling time pressure video game players number every day in possible. Also, it means that the lazy students or disliking learning students or no job people or (less working hours) part time working people, they will be the main target video game customers, due to they accept to spend much time to visit their video game shops to choose any kinds of video game softwares to buy in preference.

● How can video game advertisement method influence feeling time pressure and feeling without time pressure video game software consumer purchase purchase?

In fact, video game sellers can choose new media chnnel to advestise their new video game software products, e.g. computer online advertisemen channel, instead of video game pictures in shops, magazine, newspapers, television, radio ,cinema, public transportation tools poster traditional advertisement channels. However, computer online advertisement channel can attract many feeling learning time pressure of students consumers and feeling lack of enough rest time working people consumers to let them to choose to view their video game software advertisements from online websites at homes conveniently.

It is easy to understand , due to these feeling lack of enough learning time student video game players and feeling lack enough rest time working people video game players, they go back home after they finished learning in schools or they finished jobs in workplaces on that video game purchase planning day. After they eat their dinners, they may turn on computers to search information from internet. Suddenly, they discover some attractive video game contents photos or images are advertised from the video game seller's website or public yahoo websie , even they can choose to buy any one of these video game softwares from online shopping channel. Then, they will feel convenient to buy any one of these video game softwares from internet channel. SO, online video game advertisement will be the feeling time pressure video game players' first time contact channel at homes or the fastest advertisement contact channel to compare visiting video game store post advertisement, television , radio , magazine contact advertisement channels, when they are staying at homes.

Due to internet is popular to be used to search any information for consumers. So, the traditional magazine, newspapers, television, radio and visiting video game stores advertisement channels won't be more attractive to the feeling time pressure video game consumers . They will chooce to find any information from internet at homes in preference , when they have at least one computer to use at home, they can click website to search any information from internet easily.

The most important factor is that they can feel to spend little time to search information from internet to compare spending more time to find anywhere places whether they has magazines or book stores to sell video game magazine and newspapers publishers, radios and television won't inform them when they have video game advertisements to let they know whether what new video game softwares will promote to sell as soon as possible when they buy newspapers or turn on radios or televisions at home.

Otherwise, internet will be easy to let the feeling presure video game software consumers to know when whose liking new video content game software(s) will be promoted to sell from internet advertisement easily. Also, the feeling time presure video software consumers can choose to buy their liking video game software (s) from online shopping channel in possible if the video game seller can provide one website to let him/her to pay visa to buy and then it can deliver the video game software(s) to his/her home immediately or tomorrow or later time when the buyer's home located in overseas or far away from the video game seller's warehouse and their softwares are needed to be delivered by air plane transportation.

So, the feeling time pressure video game players won't need to leave their homes to spend more time to visit any video game stores to make final video game purchase decision any time. Hence, online advertisement and shopping channel will be one good sale promotion method to any feeling time pressure video game players nowadays. It will influence the traditional visiting video game stores' video game consumers' purchase behaviors to change to online purchase behaviors at homes conveniently, because they avoid to waste much time to visit video game stores as well as avoid to waste much time to choose any video game products in different video game stores, when they are staying in different video game stores. Visiting video game purchase behavior will need they spend whole day time to make final purchase choice, even it is possible that they can not make any video game softwares purchase decision after they visit many video game stores on that day.

Otherwise , online game advertisment channel can let them to feel to spend little time to search any new video game contents from every web page as well as every web page can show the new video game content images or photos or pictures to let every online users to see clearly when he/she sits down to turn on computer to search any kinds of video game content information to view at home in short time.

In conclusion, online video game advertisement and online shopping channel can attract many feeling time pressure video game players' consideration when they need to search any kinds of new or old video game contents information and it also changes their purchase decision to online shopping from traditonal visiting video game store shopping behavior. Video game industry's advertisement method , sale method is the kind of video game playing content's easy or difficult feeling degree , spending how much playing time to win the competiton in the game entertainment environment factors will influence the feeling time pressure video game players' final purchase decision making choice behavior to any video game software publishers nowadays.

Long time pressure brings poor performance and customer negative emotion reason

It has one interest question concerns: May salespeople ought spend long time or short time to explain the product's advantages in order to persuade customers to choose to buy the product more easily? I assume that consumers do not like to spend long time to listen any salespople to explain whether what advantages of the product has as well as they they will feel time pressure to listen any salespople explain what the product has different characteristics to compare other kinds of similar products. So, if the salespeople can spend little time to explain what the product's difference and characteristics to compare the kinds of similar products in order to let the customer feels understanding what the actual functions to product owns and what benefit it can attribute to let him to feel satisfactory when he uses the product. Then, the " less product function explanation " will achieve easily sale to cmpare " long time product function explanation". Because customers will feel time pressure when they need to spend long time to listen any salespoples' long time product function explanation in shop. I shall indicate two variable salespeople case to explain how and why they can cause extreme positive and negative emotion to their same potential vehicle customers in the shop as below:

In one car sale store, there are two salespeople, their sale skills are different. The first salesperson likes to spend long time to introduce any styles of vehicles' function to let every vehicle potential customer to know as well as he will also explain their feedbacks to let they understand their enquiries clearly. Because he believes that his vehicle potential customer will like him to introduce evey vehicle's strengths and weaknesses and unique functions to let he/she knows clearly.

He believes that he can increase any vehicle sale chance after every his potential customer can spend long time to listen his " long time product function introduction" and his plans to spend 30 minutes at least for his every time vehicle function introduction because he also believes that he can increase any styles of vehicles sale chance if his potential vehicle customers can accept to spend 30 minutes at least to listen his vehicle introduction in the car shop. He feels that his clients ought enjoy to listen his long time vehicle function introduction and they can be persuaded to buy any styls of vehicles more easily if they can attent to listen his vehicle function introduction in long time. SO, his sale skill focus on providing lot of vehicle knowledge to talk to any kinds of potential vehicle customers. They include any new styles of vehicles' relevant productive skills, characteristics , functions, strengths and weaknesses comparison to other similar styls of vehicles. He feels that they are his students and they enjoy to learn different new and old vehicles; engines comparison interestingly and they ought not feel time consumption pressure to listen his any long time vehicle function introduction talking.

Otherwise, the another vehicle salesperson does not spend long time to explain any new and old vehicle's function, characteristics and provide vehicle engine knowledge to let them to know. He feels " less time vehicle function introduction" sale skill will persuade any potential customers to choose to buy any styles of vehicles from him more easily. His sale skill focuses on following every kind of occupation to every potential customer's occupation background and making the suitable recommendation after his judgement what will be his/her preferable acceptance by his less time vehicle introduction. So, he believes that different occupation background of vehicle potential cusomer will have different vehicle driving need if he can know what kind of job he/she is doing. Then, he can follow his/her occupation need to give the persuasive and rational and reasonable recommendation concerns which kinds of styles vehicle(s) is (are) the most suitable vehicle product to let the client to drive. So, he won't spend long time to explain any styles of new and old vehicle engines and characteristics and function and compare their strengths and weaknesses to let them to know or understand clearly. He won't feel they are his students and he will not assume that they have interest to learn different styles kinds of vehicle engines knowledge.

I shall explain three kinds of different occupations vehicle potential customers how their occupations will influence their vehicle choices differently as below: As above these two vehicle salespeople. The prior one must provide not enquire what their occupations are. He must provide all new and old vehicle engine knowledge to let them to compare. Otherwise, the later one must engine what their occupations are. He must not provide all new and old vehicle engine knowledge to let them to compare, because he believes that there are not all potential vehicle customers like to compare any styles of new and old vehicle engines to make purchase choice, even purchase decision consequently.

For one engineer occupation vehicle potential customer (client) example, he will be one proficient analytical and engine calculation person. The later salesperson will provide actual data calculation evidences to let him to know. So, this engineer occupation vehicle potential client's sale chance which depends on whether how much actual engine data calculation evidences which can be provided to let him to know. Then, this potential vehicle client will follow this later vehicle salesperson his all actual engine data knowledge to attempt to calculate and judges and make subjective observsations and compares to analyze different similar styles of vehicles engine structures and characteristics as well as compares the advantages (strengths) and disadvantages (weaknesses) of these siilar styles of vehicle engines. Instead of the actual engine data knowledge provision, the later salesperson also needs to provide these data, e.g. how much oil or gas driving useful consumption expenditure for the similar styles of vehicles every driving mile, every similar styles of vehicle repair maintenance expenditure etc. actual data information.

So, the later salesperson only need to concentrate on providing these actual vehicle engine dat and energy useful and the possible maintenance expenditures to different similar styles of vehicles. He aims to let his potential vehicle client can make quality and characteristics comparison to judge whether which kind of styles of vehicle has the most excellent peformance more easily, then he can persuade him to choose to buy any kind of styles of vehicles in his car shop more easily.

Next, for another nurse occupation potential vehicle buyer example, if the later vehicle salesperson only concentrates on providing any new and old vehicle actual engineering machines data to let the nurse occupation vehicle client to know. Then, she will feel he is wasting her time or she will reject to buy any styles of vehicles from his introduction more easily. Due to her occupation is nurse, she is not proficient to engine data calculaton. She has patient respect personalty. I think that the later salesperson ought consider how to speak warmth and sympathy to let the nurse vehicle potential customer to feel his considerable vehicle introduction that he does not need to consider whether he can persuade her to buy this style of vehicle only. He can let her to feel that he is a sympathy salesperson and he respects to explain any styles of vehicles to let her to know. So, he ought let her to enquire any questions that she feels doubt concerns any styles of vehicles and he needs to concentrate explaining any answers to let her to know respectly in his whole talking time. Then, his sale chance will be increase in possible , due to her sympathetic feeling is caused from his talking and she will feel that he does not only respect that whether he can sell any vehicle from her.

Finally, for the television director occupation vehicle client example, he likes to contact any new things or know any new news and he is one owning creative mind feeling personalty. So, the later salesperson only needs to concenrate on introducing any new styles vehicles or the vehicles which general people feel difficult to find in any vehicle sale shops.

Thus, it seems that spending long time hard to introduction and providing any styles of vehicles engines knowledge sale skill can not be the most influential factor to persuade any potential vehicle clients to choose to buy this vehicle shop's any styles of vehicles more easily. Otherwise, spending less time to judgement whether what the occupation of vehicle client is and following whom occupation background and analyzing sale skill will be the suitable sale skill to persuade the vehicle client feels need to make the fast vehicle purchase desire in short time. Because different occupation working people will have different working mode or attitude as well as their working mode or attitude will influence their vehicle purchase mode or attitude from the vehicle saleperson's sale skill. So, the vehicle salespeople ought follow whom occupation mode to decide how to talk his/her vehicle sale introduction to let whose vehicle buyer to know or understand rationally. In conclusion, spending less time vehicle strategic sale introduction skill will be more suitable vehicle sale method to compare spend long time traditional providing vehicle engine data knowledge, function, characteristics , features comparison method. It seems that long time vehicle sale introduction method will let any vehicle potential clients to feel that the salesperson is wasting whose time to listen his/her talking in the vehicle shop.

Consequently, any product sale chance will be influenced by how the salesperson's sale skill, it does not consider whether how long time the sale salesperson spends to let the potential client to listen in the shop. Because it is usually that clients will feel time pressure when they need to spend long time to listen any salespeoples' talking about explaining the product in shop. It also means that they won't feel enjoy to spend long time to listen any salesperson's talking between them. So, long listening time will cause potential client feels time pressure and it will brings negative purchase emotion and they won't be persuaded to choose to buy the product by the long time talking salespeople more easily in the shop. Otherwise, speaking short talking and listening time will cause enjoyable feeling to the client and it can bring positive purchase emotion to potential client and the saleperson's talking behavior can encourage the potential client to choose to buy the kind of product more easily in the shop.

TIME PRESSURE INFLUENCE ENTREPRENEUR SUCCESS

CHAPTER SEVEN

Entrepreneurship successful factors

Entrepreneurial intentions

In the specific field of academic entrepreneurship, entrepreneurial intentions have not yet received much attention to any business creator (founder) generally. Because they were interested in combining economic and psychological approaches to get the bigger picture.

What is the economic perspective on academic entrepreneurial intention? Generally, it is important to consider economic variable when setting up a prediction model of academic entrepreneurial intentions. Entrepreneurship research already has a long tradition in studying an individual's current human capital and social capital as the affects of any entrepreneurial outcomes (i.e. one's decision to pursue an entrepreneurial career).

Human capital comprises an individual's knowledge and skills which are acquired through education, on-the job- training and other types of experiences which may increase one's productivity at work. However, from an entrepreneurial perspective, human capital is assumed to provide the (potential) entrepreneur with superior cognitive abilities regarding the exercise of demanding activities, such as starting one's own business creation.

Social capital

In the economic factors view point, the concept of social capital was originally developed in sociology. Social capital is concerned one's social ties to other individuals, groups, or organizations. Social capital resources are sourced from those ties have been shown to particularly affect the early stages of the entrepreneurial process, i.e. the initial decision to engage in entrepreneurship. Thus, the study of human and social capital may also contribute to a better understanding of academic scientist's understanding on entrepreneurship.

Human and social capital may also be to a better ability to contribution new knowledge to society. They both should have a significant bearing on the entrepreneurial career decision among scientists. Indeed, academic entrepreneurship literature emphasizes that network ties to any industrial firms to achieve an entrepreneurial career.

They can provide social and human resource network knowledge and information commercialized via entrepreneurship in economic view point. Similarly, personal entrepreneurial can experience adds to academic scientists' specific human capital by providing direct learning about the entrepreneurial process to predict whether how to decide to do any entrepreneurial activities to achieve the best way more accurate absolutely.

In fact, entrepreneurship is as an economic activity and occupational choice decision where expected benefits are central to society. In the simplest form of this model, individuals choose between starting a risky entrepreneurial behavior or working in paid employment and earning a risk-free wage as the wage is usually fixed in an employment contract. Assuming that are possesses the necessary resources to start up and given the individual risk-taking, one will choose to engage in entrepreneurship of the expected future profits from becoming an entrepreneur are larger than the sum of expected future benefits from employed work. Thus, such economic models have recently been developed to predict scientists' academic entrepreneurship.

In generally, it seems the expected entrepreneurial benefits need to be large enough to compensate for the risk-free wage in academic sector employment and for the recognition benefits of academic research. These are general economic factors influence how every individual entrepreneur's needs to create whose business in society.

On the psychological factors perspective hand, to research how influences to entrepreneurial intention issue, it concerns a widely researched psychological framework for understanding and predicting behavioral intentions is the theory of any entrepreneur individual planned behavior.

Attitude

Attitude can reflect an individual entrepreneur's behavior to evaluate whether what positive or negative psychological factors to influence the entrepreneurs how decide to choose to the behavior for whose entrepreneurial activity and the commercial use of whose research knowledge.

The social norms of science which traditionally profit making intention motives are beginning to influence to entrepreneur individual psychology. Thus, it brings this question: How does which combine the economic and psychological perspectives to influence any entrepreneur individual behavior?

In economic approach, I feel that human and social capital and expected benefits factors will influence the entrepreneur individual attitudes, perceived behavioral control and social norms of psychological factors to decide how to choose whose academic entrepreneurial intentions to do whose individual behavioral outcome to attempt to solve any barriers to achieve whose academic entrepreneurship behavior.

Thus, the psychological factors of attitudes, social norms and perceived behavioral control should be seen as entrepreneur personal intention predictors. Whereas the economic variables refer to external environment influence factors of intention predictors, so called background factors. As such background factors are proposed to affect intentions via the psychological factors. Thus, economic variable factors seem as predictors of attitudes and perceived behavioral control because I believe economic variable factors can be more influential to entrepreneur personal psychological attitude change how to decide to change whose activities to adapt any economic environment to do whose entrepreneurial intention behavior consequently. For example, background (economic) factors ,such as perceived environmental dynamism (e.g. industry opportunities) or individual skills predict corporate entrepreneurial intentions (intentions to act entrepreneurially within existing small and newly established companies) indirectly via attitudes and perceived control , but not via social norms.

Some psychological research on attitude formation identified several factors as important determinants of behavioral attitudes. For example, the entrepreneur prior behavioral experiences connected with the target behavior, either made during one's own past behavior (comparable to human capital factors) or made via networks (comparable to social capital factors) are deemed important. Thus, the entrepreneur's positive outcome expectation of beliefs about the likely consequences of a certain behavior result in positive attitudes regarding this behavior when these consequences are valued. (e.g. financial gains) are comparable to expected consequences that are indeed valued . (i.e. financial gains) are most likely seen as something positive.

Positive psychological factors

I shall indicate the psychological factors to these industries of entrepreneurs need to own, such as financial service and retail industries entrepreneurs' attitude examples as below:

Firstly, in financial service industry entrepreneurs are scored the highest in agreeableness (defined as trust, empathy, tolerance, and kindness) of the three sectors, but they were still more competitive then average for the whole sample. They were also the most emotionally stable and therefore well equipped to deal with the high-pressure nature of financial well.

Secondly, in retail sale industry, retail entrepreneurs were the most extraverted of the three sectors. By contrast, entrepreneurs in finance and technology tended to be more happy in their own company, scoring significantly high average in happy feeling. Retail entrepreneurs were also less likely to take financially risky decisions and were more luck rather than in their own ability to control external events.

Thus, it seems these both industry entrepreneurs need have these positive psychological factors to create whose new businesses of who want be one successful entrepreneur. So, their attitudes include these psychological characteristics, such as risk propensity, open, conscientiousness, extraversion, agreeableness, neuroticism, self-efficacy, autonomy need, autonomy attitude, initiative, innovativeness, achievement motivation, focus of control.

The psychology of entrepreneurship (2015) indicated the psychological data was collected from participants in four mature economies around the world to provide an international perspective on the human aspects of this balance exercise. It explained the psychological differences of entrepreneurs from the four different countries and the varying psychological drivers behind business creation in each of them. In terms of personality traits, entrepreneurs in the UK tended to be more extraverted than those in the other countries, when German entrepreneurs were the most competitive and the most emotionally stable. German entrepreneurs were not found to be any more conscientious then those in the UK or USA. So, it means different country entrepreneurs will have similar psychology of personality traits to the country's entrepreneurs' characteristics generally as well as it is possible that every country's economic environment (background) factor won't influence why the country's entrepreneur's individual behavior who have similarity generally. Thus, it concludes every country economy environment (background) factor can influence the country's entrepreneur's individual behavior choice possibly.

How factors influence the differences between small-scale and large scale business performance. Some entrepreneurship psychologists indicate factors can influence the differences between small scale and large scale business performance, due to the differences in behavior of entrepreneur and individual's access to strategic resource and socialization process.

Buttner & Makhbul (2011) explained factors influence business performance includes among many others: their professional background, their entrepreneurship capabilities and performance preferences, cultural and beliefs, as well as the technology and micro-environment.

However, I feel the rate of similarities of large or small scale business failure continues to increase because of the obstacles affecting business performance which include: lack of financial resources, lack of management experience, poor location and marketing promotion , low and regulations banned, general economic conditions, as well as critical factors, such as poor infrastructure, corruption, low demand for products and services and poverty. Other factors include storage of raw materials, handicap in obtaining finance, inadequate competent personnel, inability to control costs and problems of dumping of cheap foreign products and others , e.g. difficult to entry the new (old) market, limited access to other enterprises and lack of employment opportunities from labor market supply or lack of attractive treatment from the entrepreneurship. Thus, what factors influence the performance differences small and large scale enterprises. How to determine greatest obstacles and challenges for the operators of small scale businesses to improve effective small scale business development to expand to large scale enterprises.

There is no single criterion for classifying business enterprises as small as medium or large scale globally. However, reference is usually made to some quantity measures such as: number of people employed by the enterprise investment outlay, the annual turnover (sales) and the asset value of the enterprise or a combination of these measures.

Generally, small or medium scale enterprises include the production of light consumer products that are primary related to food and beverages, clothing, electrical parts,, automotive parts, manufacture, leather product, soap and detergents, woodworks. Small scale businesses are divided into three sectors: production sector of agricultural processing, manufacturing, and mining . Service sectors and trading sector including wholesales and retails.

The purpose to examine factors influence performance of both small and medium scale businesses . Thus, what variable factors can influence small or medium scale businesses. An increasing number of psychologists believed that motivation and goals of an entrepreneur affect business performance. The motivation of an entrepreneur determines success of such from small scale to medium scale entrepreneurs. The reasons to motivate entrepreneur, it is possible that because of economic status and survival. Thus, motivation is as a factor shows a strong relation to business performance. The financial resources challenges will influence entrepreneur's effort of motivation include: inability to control costs, inadequate competent staff and problems of policies, incentives and operation etc. financial challenges factors.

In conclusion, however, entrepreneur's goals and motivation will influence whose business performance from small scale to medium scale to large scale expansion for whose entrepreneurship growth for long term.

Motivation factors influence entrepreneurs on business surviving

What are the major impact of motivation factors influence entrepreneurs on business surviving. Entrepreneurship is a significant factors for economic growth, innovation and job creation of countries. This ensures a positive motivation to entrepreneurs. Thus, it brings this question: What is/are the major positive motivation factors to influence entrepreneurs success?

I shall recommend a new categorization for motivational variables was designed in order to deliver a new explanation of the major motivational structure of successful entrepreneurs.

In psychological view point, the major motivation factors ought include: independence, financial reward, social recognition and need for achievement. Also, those psychological factors will have on a variety of indicators for any business, surviving success and impact financial performance absolutely.

I shall explain to indicate my reason why I feel that the desire for independence has the most significant and strongest influence on the financial performance. The motivation for financial reward has a negative influence on the financial performance. Business surviving for social recognition has a significant long term influence need for achievement has an influence on the growth of sales, but not on the return on sales.

This research on the motivations of people to start a business has a significant impact on the understanding what major factors influence the entrepreneurs decide to choose to do the activities for whose business survival. However, the major motivation factors only include psychology and economy two aspects to influence any entrepreneurs' activities absolutely. For example, of the economic development is driven by a further effect of new enterprises. Though the creation of a new firm, competitors as well as large and long existing companies have to improve themselves. So they won't disappear from the market easily. Thus, entrepreneurs' attitude is a major factor to influence business success. In general, in small companies, the relationships between the variable of the individual and the variables of the company are stronger than in large enterprises. The reason is because the motivation of any small company entrepreneurs play a crucial role when all environmental influences are held constant more than large company entrepreneurs in societies.

The importance of motivation of the entrepreneur in relation to the establishment of a company which concern different reasons influences. For example, the expected return on sales growth factor, expected business survival factor, entrepreneur personal interesting reasons. Then, entrepreneurship can be classified into three categories. The first category is the behavior of an entrepreneur and what who do. The second category consists of the question: What happens when entrepreneurs are and what is the result of these actions. The last category examines the fact, why people decide to become an entrepreneur and what motivates people to become an entrepreneur.

In order to promote the economic development of a country by creating the right environment for entrepreneurship. Thus, good economy environment will have a high probability to let them to establish a successful business. In contrast, economic unsuccessful business. In contrast, economic unsuccessful new ventures will have resources as well as skillful workers shortages to the entrepreneurs to satisfy their needs an the labor market.

There are two interesting questions: Do various motivation structures of entrepreneurs have a differential effect on the business surviving success of new business companies? Which motivating factor has a significant impact on financial performance of any founded company?

To answer these two questions, I shall suppose that the various motivational factors of the entrepreneurs have a differential impact on any business surviving success is founded enterprises, the more the entrepreneur is motivated by financial rewards and/or by need for achievement and/or by social recognition and/or by the desire for independence when starting the better business success. Thus, I believe the relationship between the motivation and development of any one founded company is based on the intentions which provides a linkage between motivation and behavior of the entrepreneur.

Why people decide to become an entrepreneur and what motivates people to become an entrepreneur. Hence in this process, the entrepreneur invests the necessary time and effort and takes financial, psychological and social risks. The entrepreneur ties to achieve financial rewards and personal social risks . The entrepreneur tries to achieve financial rewards and personal satisfaction. Through this process as well as entrepreneurship is as a process of understanding evaluating and exploiting of business opportunities in order to convert them into services and products.

However, I believe these external and internal factors which have an influence to any company's founding process. The external include the state of economic environment, in which the company was founded, competitors, government regulations and technological progress. In addition to the external circumstances, internal factors of the company founder play a role when starting a business, such as how starting a business , such as how chosen strategy of the company founder, the decisions taken and the management style as factors that will determine the success of a business. In addition to these factors, internal factors also include personality, cognitive, skills, network, professional and industrial experience of the entrepreneur.

Consequently, I believe above these external economic environment factors as well as internal founder psychological factors which will influence the business founder to decide motivate whose business in whose entrepreneurial foundation process generally.

Entrepreneurship innovation and economy growth influence to entrepreneurs

Concept innovation factor

The definition of the concept innovation are clearly relationship to influence to entrepreneur psychology. It concerns these questions: How do entrepreneurship innovations which come about and by whom? , i.e. the connection to entrepreneurial activities. What way does innovation contribute to new knowledge through scientific/technical discoveries? Which knowledge bases and cognitive abilities are critically important for innovation to take place? How does innovation substantiate into growth? Which policy measures should be taken in order to boost the probability of sustained knowledge based growth?

Nowadays, economic-based theories and models largely fall short of addressing to important economic outcomes. For example, the accumulation of factors of production, i.e. knowledge, human and/or physical capital can't alone explain economic development. Innovation and entrepreneurship are needed to input in profitable ways. Thus, it brings this question: How does successful new enterprise t the micro level to transfer into economic progress at the social level and for a failed entrepreneurship at the micro level to contribute to economic development ? However, the societal implications of the actions of individual entrepreneurs, i.e. how that translates into growth and prosperity is thus not fully considered.

I feel knowledge is important to any entrepreneur because knowledge generation and exploitation. Have the financial systems by evaluation prospective entrepreneurs, mobilizing and channeling savings to finance the most productivity-enhancing activities, diversifying risks, etc. play a vital role. Thus, the question is how that is accounted for in standard knowledge driven growth models.

How to avoid uncertain and risky outcomes

Why do individuals engage in entrepreneurial ventures with uncertain and risky outcomes? To answer this question, we need to know innovation contains elements of risk also for the entrepreneurs. In fact, the role of the entrepreneur is as someone who transforms uncertainty into a calculable risk. Thus, the uncertainty and risk to the entrepreneur may include that what innovation is perceives and creates new opportunities, how and why operates under uncertainty and introduces products to the market, decision on location, and hoe manages whose businesses and the for and use of resources and competes with others for a share of the market.

Can entrepreneurships influence economic growth? we can view this case from the distribution between supply side and demand side to force seem somewhat. Is for instance, unemployment a variable that can be derived from the demand or the supply side of the economy? Notwithstanding that the distinction between demand and supply side factors may be imprecise. Among these are knowledge and how it ties in with human capital and knowledge resources. However, there will always be limitations in accessing knowledge. Measures concerning access and level of knowledge tend likewise to be partial. Indeed , even if the total stock of knowledge were freely available, knowledge about its existence would not necessary be. So, how higher rates of entrepreneurship knowledge in to innovations and set forces if it is creative destruction into motion which will be considered to any entrepreneurship. For example, how to define and measure innovation? According to Schumpeter (1911/340 is explicit about the economic function of the entrepreneurs, who indicated the process of economic development could be divided into three clearly separate stages. The first stage implies technical discovery of new things or new ways of things, who refers to as invention. In the subsequent stage innovation occurs, i.e. the successful commercialization of a new good or service from technical discoveries or more generally, a new combination of knowledge (new or old). The final step in this three stages process imitation concerns a more general adoption of new products or processes to markets. Schumpeter has also clear about the difference between roles played by the inventor and compared to the innovator.

Thus, the hypothesis is that entrepreneurship is linked to economic growth finds its most immediate foundation in simple, intuition, common sense and pure economic observation, activities to convert ideas into economic opportunities. So, it feel entrepreneurship is source of innovation and change, and as such improvement, innovation and change, and as such improvement in productivity and economic competitiveness with technological change and the global competition brought about by globalization and economic liberalization, the assumption that entrepreneurship means global innovation and economy competition or development to every entrepreneur nowadays.

Thus, it brings these questions: What is the exact nature of entrepreneurship and it's role in economic theory? What are the links of entrepreneurship to economic growth? Can entrepreneurship b considered as the interface between small business (the micro level) and economic growth (the macro level)?

Most economic , psychological and sociological research points to the fact that entrepreneurship is a process and not a static phenomenon. Entrepreneurship is more than just economic factor (Pirich 2001, 14-15). Entrepreneurship has to do with change and is also commonly associated with choice-related issues.

In conclusion, how economy influences entrepreneurship development, I feel that when developing economies grow as standard economic growth models, predict through the accumulation of human and physical capital and increasing specialization: Once an economy has entered the industrialized phase of capitalist development , a qualitative change in the driver of economic growth occurs. In advanced industrial economies, growth is driven by the process of technological advance and knowledge accumulation brought by research and development efforts of firms consequently. Thus, finally, every entrepreneur needs to judge to apply different strategies to attract consumer psychological change to choose to buy whose products or consume whose services as well as how to already to adapt economic change influences to develop whose entrepreneurship in long term.

Reference

Buttner, E. H. (2011) Examing female entrepreneur management style: An application of a relational frame. Journal of business ethics. 29(3) . pp. 253-269.

Makhbul, Z.M. (2011) Entrepreneurial success: An

exploratory study among entrepreneurs. International journal of business management vol. 1 (6). pp. 1-10.

Schumpeter, J., (1911/34) , The theory of economic development , Harvard University press, Cambridge, Ma. The psychology of entrepreneurship , June 2015, pp.10

Time queue pressure brings theme park entertainment industry visitors negative emotion

For theme park entertainment industry, when visitors enter to any entertainment theme park , they need to queue to wait long time to play any entertainment machine facilities, which will bring their negative emotions and it can influence they feel not choose to go to the entertainment theme park to play any entertainment machine facilites again. Then, it will be possible to reduce the entertainment theme park visitors number because they can choose another entertainment theme park to replace it. I shall indicate Walt Disney entertainment theme park case example to explain how it avoids visitors feel long time queue pressure to influence their positive entertainment emotion during they are staying in Disney.

In the past Disney background history, Disney had encountered human resource and strategic management etc. different challenges about ten years. How to design its entertainment facilities to attract many visitors to visit and let they feel no any queue time pressure when they have interest to play any entertainment facilities, due to global entertainment theme park competitors are increasing, how to change its image to let visitors to feel it has much different image to compete its competitors. I shall explain how and why Disney needs to arrange entertainment facilities management to avoid any visitors feel time pressure when they need to queue to play as below:

First, what is a tourist destination and space tourist destination difference? e.g. space trip routes, Disney trip routes. Because any Disney visitors can not play all entertainment facilities and visit any entertainment destination in one day as well as any space travellers can not catch the space ship to fly all routes in space in one day. Hence, any Disney entertainment theme park and space tourism companies need provide any suitable space tourism destinations or Disney entertainment facilities destinations to let consumers to choose to entertain.

A tourism destination has many different characteristics. It is one product but also many,

involves many stakeholders with differing objectives and requirements, is both a physical entity and a socio-cultural one, is a mental concept for potential tourists, is subject to the influence of current events, natural disasters, terrorism, health scares etc.is subject to historical, real and fictitious events,

is evaluated subjectively in respect of its value-for-money (based on reality compared with expectations), and differs in size, physical attractions, infrastructure, benefits offered to visitors and degree of dependence on tourism ? In fact no two tourism destinations can be treated the same. Disney ought to choose space travel feactures to attract many visitors, so it ought no choose general earth tourism features because space tourism features are more attractive and fresh ideas to attract visitors, e.g. space toursim related entertainment facilities, space tourism 3 D to 5 D movies to provide visitors to watch to feel who are sitting in space flying boats to travel during they are staying Disney theme park any time. So, they will feel Disney theme park is one space tourism boat similarly.

Second, what are between space tourism impacts and Disney entertainment impacts difference ? Tourism has a far wider range of direct and indirect impacts than other economic sectors. At its simplest tourism can be seen to be a temporary addition to the population of a given location, with tourists having all the needs and impacts that the permanent population does, plus a few more besides. Government planning, regulation etc. is therefore needed; yet tourism is an economic sector executed by the private sector. Tourism activity involves direct contact with the local population. Tourism, then, involves a triumvirate of destination interests ?state, private sector and community.

As such, Disney must let visitors to feel that it can provide space tourism service to let they to play in short time , it is not general tourism servic to satisfy their space toursim entertinment theme park difference. Space tourism planning for development and marketing is unlike any other economic sector and requires special approaches, procedures and institutions. Thus, Disney needs to know that space tourism features are different to general earth tourism as well as what factors will influence whose consumers do not choose to find their entertainment service. e.g. expensive air ticket, too cold or too hot weather, expensive space ship tickets or Disney admission fee , crowd in Disney or space ship etc. different factors to influence whose customers' choices.

Third, what is the difference between general earth tourism and space travel tourism perception? ?what is reality? How between space and earth tourism difference between a destination, or commercial tourism organisation, promotes its products and/or services is a key factor in the realisation of developmental or economic/financial objectives. In an activity like earth tourism where the customer is so far to live from the place he/she is considering to visit. Otherwise, on space tourism perception and reality hand, such as spending long time to catch plan to arrive Disney or space ship destination or what entertainment service he/she is thinking to buy, such as Disney entertainment facilities or space ships facilities. Disney space entertainment tourism marketing is a central component of tourism. Two of the adages of tourism marketing arising from this situation are that:

(1) Disney cannot test drive a earth holiday only? and it ought let its visitors to feel space tourism hoilday in short time enjoyable entertainment feel, such as they can feel that they are sitting rockets to fly to moon to travel in short time.

(2) On Disney short time space tourism, the perception is the reality to its visitors' space tourism feeling in short time?

Disney long time wait queue pressure problem

Wiig, k.(1993) indicated that The Walt Disney Company is one of the largest media and entertainment corporation in the world. Founded on Oct. 16, 1923 by brothers Walt and Roy Disney as a small animation studio. Today, it is one of the largest Hollywood Studios and also owns eleven theme parks, two water parks and several television networks, including the American broadcasting company. Disney entertainment theme park expansion has in recent years focused heavily on Asia, and specifically China, Hong Kong, Japan.

What factors caused Walt Disney strategic and human resource problems ?

In the beginning, Disney underestimated and neglected some strategic and organizational behavior issues which can influence its different departments' operations inefficiently. What factors caused Walt Disney human resource and hotel operational problems?

On the human resource problem hand, Bahandin, G et al., (2009) indicated that" errors are made regarding overall operation for Euro Disneyland from its American experience that Disney throughout Monday would be the light day for guests and Friday would be a heavy day to allocate staffs. In fact to this day, it had not enough staff to supply to staffing at a theme park, where the number of visitors per day in the high season can be 10 times the number in the low season ; wrong operational assumption of bus driver, it built the French bus parking space much too small. Bus drivers were unhappy as they had a very difficult time fitting their buses into their designated spots. In addition, Disney provided only 50 restroom facilities for bus drivers and on peak days there would be 2000 drivers ; operational errors are made to computer involved stations at the hotels. It assumed guests would stay at the park for morning spent the day at the park checked into the hotel late that night, and then checked out early the next morning before heading back to the park. Since there were so many guests checking in and checking out, additional computer station had to be installed at the hotels in order to decrease the amount of time the guests stood in line and hotel counter service staff numbers would also need to be increased. "

On the hotel operation problem hand, Dickson et al.,(2005) also indicated that" it had wrong belief that it understood European breakfast taste and Disney was told Europeans didn't eat sit down breakfast. This resulted in Disney downsizing their restaurants before Euro Disneyland opened. In fact, they were trying serve 2500 breakfasts in a 350 seat restaurant at some of the hotels. Further guests wanted bacon and eggs rather than just coffee. Disney reacted quickly with pre-packaged breakfast delivered to rooms and satellite. Thus, it caused result in Disney downsizing their restaurants."

The reasons showed that French Disney restaurants are caused to fail , such as lacked French cultural characteristics, but only European social and eating pattern ; the non availability of alcohol proved, employees were not expected to be spoken in French language and who also were not fluent in English. Hence, Disney restaurants can not accept French eating style and culture to attract many French visitors to go to Disney restaurants to eat.

Due to, USA Disney did not follow French people eating taste and speaking cultural, It must cause its French restaurant operation unsuccessfully before.

In addition, Disney has wrong judgement to operate its business in USA and overseas Disney operation wrongly. Such as Disney estimated the demand of employee numbers wrongly. It only employed an additional 200 experienced Disney managers were located in the other three centres. In addition, some 4000 employees were unable to find suitable positions. It caused management lacks optimistic assumptions to know who ought to be provided training to its staffing to dealt cultural difference challenges. Moreover, it also had external threats and internal weakness challenges. It included high bank investment interest rates charge , unreasonable working conditions, poor communication and lack of cultural awareness because managers and it caused staff turnover increasing finally. The most failure, before Disney had not carrying on research whether whose visitors feel happy and satisfactory to enjoy its entertainment facilities when who are staying in Disney. Otherwise, who feel unsatisfactory and unhappy , even who need to complaint whose service quality. Hence, Disney numbers of visitors was decreasing before. Such as, visitors felt unhappy because who need to spent much time to queue. It also caused Disney visitor numbers was declining. Thus, Disney will need to consider how to change human resource activities to adapt clients' needs, such as reducing bad emotion to cause visitors who needed to spend much time to queue to wait to play entertainment facilities.

Disney traditional knowledge management strategy

Disney had attempted this traditional knowledge management strategy to solve its human resource and daily business operation challenges successfully. As Harriet Griffey (2010) stated that "sometimes, boredom can give disadvantages to reduce staffs' ability to motive to work and reduces positive emotion , such as happiness. Thus, it causes people (staffs) lack motivated reasoning to unconsciously evaluate evidence in ways consistent with whose preferences. This type of bias can hinder a company's ability to learn from mistakes and to build successful strategies."

However, Disney chose to implement knowledge management strategy to satisfy visitors demands and needs to let who feel more satisfactory when who entered Disney to play its any entertainment as below:

For first example, Disney demanded cleaners to repeat to remember any information to prepare to answer visitors' enquiries. It will train every cleaner memory to remember any information to be long term from short term memory successfully and every cleaner won't feel bore to do only cleaning job duty. When every one feel places are clean, who will concentrate on answering any visitors enquiries as the same time. Even, if they can give excellent service performance to serve visitors to let who to know how to go to any places in the short time. It is possible that visitors will appreciate whose service performance to let their manager to know, so that every cleaner will have chance to raise salary.

Besides for second example, waiting time and queues are daily problem for Disney theme park. Fast lines or priority queues appear as a solution of efficient queues for clients. Disney understood fast ticket line system affected visitor attendance numbers. Disney entertainment facilities long waits leaded to lower service evaluations and greater customer dissatisfaction. Efficient queue waiting time management can improve Disney visitor satisfaction and the willingness to recommend the service. Disney analysed of theme park visitor behaviour in relation to pay the higher ticket price to select to pay more for fast queuing line ticket than common queuing line ticket. In fact, Disney fast queuing line ticket system choice gave potential queues to any waiting clients . In general, Disney visitors don't like to wait long time in every entertainment facilities queuing line, who will feel a waste of time and waiting can lead to negative emotional response like frustration, impotence, tension or irritation .

In fact, Disney amusement theme park needed visitors wait long queues and delays which were a frequent occurrence in every entertainment facilities line. Disney theme park as sets of rides, spectacles and leisure mechanisms are intended to entertainment and spark the imagination of clients, allowing visitors to escape their daily routing. In result, waiting is often a problematic issue that can influence Disney visitor experience and that can appear as one of the principal motives for complaining. As Disney visitor demand fluctuates constantly and demand patterns are often difficult to predict. It caused extra staff needed for the extra line. Finally, priority services such as fast line system facilities segmentation of its amusement park. When Disney offer the possibility of purchases a fast line, which are creating two different group. Disney visitors who are highly sensitive to waiting times are willing to pay to avoid or reduce lines or visitors that are highly sensitive to price that prefer to wait rather than to pay extra money.

Also, Disney provides extensive training opportunity for participants through its own Disney university. The question of whether their training opportunity can lead the improve human resource activities. On the third hand problem, Disney are also worried that employees may leave it and join other competitor to serve their parks after training. Disney shows a trend of increasing depending on human capital other than physical capital. It thinks human capital is the knowledge, skills, ideas and commitment of its employees. It explains that investing in training and development is essential to its client service growth. In fact, Disney had owned enough entertainment facilities, restaurants, hotels, shopping centres within thcme park, but its visitor numbers are increasing to need to be served satisfactorily. However, it needs to train cleaners, entertainment facilities service staffs, queuing service staffs, hotels, restaurants, shopping centres service staffs, instead of it's entertainment facilities attraction.

For the final example, Disney observes that spending on training and development is typically regarded as consumption, instead of investment. On job training usually can't be replaced by formal education, therefore Disney chooses to make contribution on providing further training and development to employees. Disney paid salary for staff training, which included classroom, seminars, symposia or conferences; computer based training, on site training, book and periodicals reading, formal mentoring and informal mentoring program opportunities to meet its old staffs and new staffs both needs of motivate factors to achieve advancement , achievement, personal growth responsibility and achievement and recognition to raise its business performance effectively and efficiently.

However, Disney's amount of training has a positive influence on intrinsic motivation of its employees. Job satisfaction, salary, working condition, its policies, administration, relationship with supervisors, peers and subordinates are Disney factors to influence it's human resource activities performance. Disney training contents include these functional area: Raising excellent service performance include that hotel food and beverage service delivery, shopping center, merchandise sale, restaurant service, entertainment facilities queuing waiting service, cleaning and enquiring how to go different locations in Disney, cashier service etc. They are very important to influence visitor numbers. Disney implementation of knowledge management solution to improve queuing waiting line process. The use of Disney front line service staffs as human capital combined with knowledge of customer preference has made the fast pass an innovation solution to enhance queuing in the Disney theme parks. Disney ability to capture customers in virtual queues when giving them a pleasurable waiting experience has made them a leader in knowledge management initiatives in the service industry. Disney's emphasis on human capital within their theme parks, combined with traditional queuing theory to create more pleasurable waiting environments. Hence, Disney showed the value of tacit employee knowledge integrated with traditional queuing theory to reduce loss of customer satisfaction to enhance, goodwill and profitability. Knowledge management expresses itself as human action in form of evaluation, attitudes, points of view, commitments, motivation etc. It seemed that Disney agreed that human capital (people, knowledge, ideas, creativity) maybe today's most valuable commodity.

How to apply knowledge management strategy to solve Disney long time queue waiting playing challenges? Knowledge Management Strategy was used to queue control from Disney. Disney managers have long understand the pressure of waiting time and revenue; who know that every minutes spent waiting in queuing is a minute that the client is not generating revenue. So, Disney managers have processed with design of a reservation system recognizes that guests can be freed from physically standing in the actually and perception of waiting by allowing guests to engage has arrived. Cope et al., (2008) showed that" the system was first tested at Disney in 1998. Managers assessed the system by surveying guests who used it. Results were positive and indicated that guests spent substantially less time in queuing, spent more per capita, and saw significantly more attractions, satisfaction level sky rocketed.The system was expanded in 1999 to include five of the most popular park attractions and was named FASTPASS. The system has since been expanded to all Disney theme parks worldwide, and is now in use by over 50 million guests per year .That guests have two options .Namely, they can choose to Obtain a FASTPASS ticket and come back a later, designed time or Wait in a traditional queuing. Guests are assisted in making their choice by information regarding estimated waits of both options. Thus, can decide to wait in the traditional queuing, or take a FASTPASS ticket and return it a later time with no further wait. Once an assigned FASTPASS time is generated and provided to a guest, it is valid for the 60 minutes beyond that time, creating a window in which guest can return."
There are numerous benefits in allowing park guests to return to an attraction within a designed time frame. Queue Waits involve managing two

major client issues:

1.How long Disney visitors actually wait every time queue.
2.How long Disney visitor think they are waiting by whose psychological feeling every time queue.

Thus, if they feel that who spend much time to queue, it will cause they feel angry and they also feel admission ticket price is paid too high to them unfairly. In general, clients were allowed the ability to see two attractions during the time they would have previously been able to see only one. This can viewed as an implementation of a multi-phased system, depending on the attraction picked, each queuing may be single channel attractions, the guest creates whose own multi phase system. Obvious, results, were that guests were able to engage in more revenue producing activities, saw more of the popular attractions and began to par take care, in other less utilized attractions .

Wiig defined(1993)" Knowledge management in different ways and from different perspective. The emphasis is on human know how and how it brings value to an organization. Intangible asset contributes to corporation objective may be immeasurable and isn't simple to evaluate the impacts of knowledge management."

However, Knowledge management may not be only factor influencing organizational performance. In fact, Disney refined technology utilization to improve the user design of all human resource related systems, improving timeliness (queue waiting time deduction), setting elapsed time goals and monitor performance towards those standards, considering to use of automated fast queue waiting system, evaluating staffing levels, a close examination of adequacy of current staff level is warranted, beyond to improve visitors satisfaction. Clients holding fast pass tickets may choose to visit a gift shop or any park concessions. Thus, Disney has ability to co-branded products and service.

Disney's approach combining queuing and human capital. Dunn, J et al., (2002) showed "The use of fast pass provides an insightful application of the combination of techniques of queuing and human capital to strategically leverage knowledge management principle .When waiting lines are an part of the Disney experience, park guests build magical memories through innovation. It is Disney's recognition of front line service staffs that transforms that employees into knowledge who multi task in their roles. For example, an attraction host or a street sweeper may be a valuable Source knowledge to park guests. In addition to their primary roles, they may have a wealth of information about attractions for guests. They may be able to give directions, provide schedules, and offer helpful suggestions from their daily observation. This is the first stop to increase knowledge management . Next, Disney improves its clients' perception by minimizing the perception of waits. The use of the fast pass enables Disney not only to enhance the psychological aspect of waiting lines, but also to capitalize at the same time." Instead, Disney needed to give people specific tools designed to help them to do their job and solve specific business problems. Thus, after Disney learned how it applied the knowledge management method to solve its challenges, e.g. Human capital and queuing theory provide two very different valuable assets to raise its competitive ability. Then, its visitor numbers was increasing largely and quickly.

In conclusion, Disney need to change it's strategy to adapt any the business environmental situation change in different time. For example, in the past, due to Disney had encountered operation challenge and human resource management challenge. So, it apply fast queue knowledge management strategy to solve visitors' spending long queue time is needed to wait to play any Disney entertainment facilities to let them feel satisfactory and feel no angry to compaint Disney. It seems that it is more successful to attract many visitors prefer to pay admission fee to visit Disney to play.

However, nowaday, Disney is encountering another kind of challenge, such as how to let visitors feel that they can spend long time to enjoy any long time and expensive similar entertainment feeling, such as sitting rockets to fly to moon travel feeling. I shall recommend that it can apply space tourism strategy to design its entertainment facilities are similar to space tourism entertainment facilities to let its visitors feel that they can spend short time to sit rockets to travel to moon.

Disney space tourism, is the perception the reality to its visitors' short time flying to moon travel feeling?

Why will Disney entertainment theme park space tourism entertainment facilities attract many visitors?

In fact, space tourism and Disney theme park both businesses which have similar characteristics. Such as they are entertainment business, Disney provides different kind of entertainment facilities to let visitors to play to feel exciting satisfaction as well as space tourism provides one space ship to let travellers spend less time to sit in the space ship to fly to space to see any space stars and let them to feel exciting in the black space environment. They have these similar aspects:

They need have high technological machine facilities to supply, e.g. Disney needs different kinds of machine entertainment facilities to let visitors to sit down to play, Space tourism needs space ships to supply to travellers to sit down to fly to space. They needs to provide high quality of entertainment service to satisfy consumer individual need, e.g. Disney needs often to change its entertainment facilities to let visitors can play any different kinds of new entertainment machines more satisfactory. Otherwise, space tourism needs often to change new design of space ships to let travellers to sit as well as chooses different space trip routes to let travellers to see different space sightseeing when their space ships enter to any different space trip route every time. Due to Disney and space tourism have these kind of similar entertainment factors to cause their business can be success or failure. Thus, I believe Disney knowledge management strategy is similar to space tourism business. I shall indicate these knowledge management strategies which can be applied to space tourism business as below:

When discussing the advancement of space science and space technology, most people think about deep space flights, lunar stations, and thrilling outer space adventures. The fact is that the majority of the human technology in space, which consists of interconnected satellites, points towards Earth, and is used to provide services for and fulfil the goals of people on planet Earth. Over the next decade, there will be an increased need for innovative Earth information systems to support the international space community's efforts to provide a robust infrastructure.

However, space exploration requires vast sums of money. Is the amount of money spent on space research justifiable? Could the money be cheaper spent to let every space travellers? Thus, space tourism will have the effective knowledge management strategy to let every space traveller to feel every space trip fee is very reasonable to satisfy their space trip needs. The space trip service includes many different kinds of space good tasty foods supplies, comfortable and good design and safe environment of space ship facilities, exciting different space trip route choices, the reasonable space trip time length, space flight timetable arrangement, space ship service attendant attitude and performance and space tourism professional technical knowledge. Thus, space tourism business needs have these unique space knowledge management knowledge: Such as space tourism service attendant staff individual space ship service knowledge and space ships safe flight and trip space science tourism knowledge, space foods manufacturing knowledge, space ships repair and crisis management knowledge. If any space tourism company expected whose space travelers have confidence to choose to sit their space ships to go to space to travel safely. Otherwise, even although if the space tourism ticket fee is cheap in common , global space travelers won't prefer to choose to catch any space ships to go to space to travel if who felt any space ships were unsafe and dangerous transportation machine to let they lack confidence to sit safely. Thus, space tourism operators need to consider how to apply knowledge management strategy to let space travelers feel more safe and satisfactory needs more than Disney visitor.

Disney short time entertainment enjoyable feeling
strategy

Disney and space tourism entertainment businesses can consider how marketing policy and strategy might be incorporated in a destination overall Disney space tourism theme park development approach, Disney needs to consider those basic characteristics of space tourism that have implications for the marketing function.

● Fragmentation of space tourism supply

The space tourist product is a composite one, a combination of attractions, transport, accommodation, entertainment and other services. In most countries, there are many separate suppliers of these various components ? Disney theme park needs to supply these unique space toursim characteristics to feel visitors to feel, such as Disney own airlines to be supplied to overseas visitors to fly to Disney by cheap airline ticket fees, Disney supplies space unique characteristics hotels which can let visitors to live in space , space tour excursion organisers supply to let visitors feel Disney is one space entertainment theme park to provide space facilities entertainment services etc.

It is an important feature of Disney space tourism concept that, though an Disney individual supplier of different Disney space entertainment tourist services may serve unique similar space entertainement facilities and space entertainment service than other similar entertainment theme park competitors market, rarely, if ever, does a single space entertainment supplier provide the entire range of Disney space similar products /space similar services required by a tourist on a visit to any destinations in space theme park. Whether sold as a Disney space entertainment cheap package or assembled by the tourist himself or by a Disney space travel agent to give cheaper Disney admission fee price to compare to other travel agent Disney ticker prices , the Disney space tourist product is in practice a composite one. It is apparent, then, that given the fragmented nature of supply on one hand, and the demand for a combined set of Disney space tourism products on the other, a fundamental challenge for a destination is to achieve coordination and integration of all components across all sub-sectors of the Disney theme park entertainment tourism industry - that is, of only one supply to Disney space tourism entertainment theme park only. So, global theme park visitors only feel only Disney theme park can provide unique space toursim feeling when they choose to enter Disney theme park. It means that other global theme entertainment theme park can not provide space tourism experiences to attract them to visit.

● Interdependence and complementarity of Disney space tourism tourist services

It follows from the fact that Disney space entertainment theme park tourism demand is for a composite product that the various general earth tourist products and services are interdependent and complementary. Disney needs to supply the unique space tourism experience to let theme park visitors to feel. The supply of one (for example Disney space tourism theme park international air transport to/from a destination) depends on the supply of another (such as hotel accommodation) and they complement each other. I means that Disney can build one airport which can let visitors to feel it has space travel feeling during they arrive the Disney country.

A Disney space tourism theme park destination reputation can be set by the weakest link in the tourist product chain. This leads to the marketing policies and actions of one enterprise directly influencing other enterprises. A country with a liberal charter policy and/or an airline with an aggressive pricing policy may result in the attraction of low budget tourists, something that could damage the high quality image central to the marketing of a five-star hotel chain in the Disney destination. There is again then the need for coordination and cooperation in order to enhance the effectiveness of individual marketing and promotional efforts of the various tourism suppliers. Due to Disney can have any space tourism airports in every country to let visitors to feel that it is only Disney visitors have qualification to enter to Disney space tourism airports only. So, any non visiting Disney theme park visitors won't have chance to enter Disney space tourism airports when they fly to the owned Disney theme park countries.

In consequence of the intangibility of Disney and space entertainment businesses are tourist entertainment service products, when a supplier of a tourist services considers the potential market, the essential thought process should be: expectations ?experiences ?memories. This is the same whether the supplier is a destination promotion authority seeking to attract tourists to a specific country or location within that country, or the operator of a fixed-site facility like a hotel, restaurant or attraction, or a provider of tour excursion.

Each Disney tourist is a set of expectations. The Disney space tourism product cannot be test driven or known about with certainty in advance of being consumed. The Disney space entertainment tourist therefore builds mental images of the destination and of the facilities and other components of the tourism product of that destination. He/she has a set of expectations about the place to be visited.

Disney space tourism experiences is because the intangibility of tourism products means that the tourist engages in a series of activities ?typically, for example, riding on Disney transport is supplied between airport and Disney theme park, Disney space entertainment facilities visiting attractions, staying in some form of space tourism accommodation, eating, drinking, recreating, interacting with other people ?none of which produce a final physical product to take home. Each Disney space tourism tourist trip, therefore, is a combination of various experiences.

At then end of the trip the tourist is left with nothing more than memories ?the derivation of the word souvenirs - and proxies of the trip ?such as supplying Disney space tourism photos or videos to let visitors who can remember when they visit to Disney to play to feel space tourism experience.

The key for the Disney space tourism marketer is that the expectations created achieve the fine balance between attracting the Disney space tourist while not promising more than can be delivered. The Disney space tourism entertainment experiences are assessed by the tourist against his/her pre-trip expectations. A major determinant of success is how well the experiences match or exceed these expectations. This assessment has relative as well absolute dimensions. A destination may have a perception in the marketplace of being expensive or offering poor service, something which will limit its drawing power. If the Disney tourist finds it is not so costly or that service is better than expected, his/her level of satisfaction will be higher. Of course, the reverse can also be the case with more damaging consequences for the destination.

The intangibility of the Disney theme park tourist product and the consequent need for the marketer to address the potential market perceptions of the tourist product has two dimensions: first, the need to offer unique space tourism psychological benefits to the prospective Disney tourist; and, second, to recognise that the perception is the space tourism reality - with each Disney tourist having sovereign power over his/her destination decision making ?and that Disney space product sale marketing activities should be designed to alter the market prevailing images in line with the marketer desired position.

Disney short time knowledge management strategy

As Harriet Griffey (2010) stated that "sometimes, boredom can give disadvantages to reduce staffs' ability to motive to work and reduces positive emotion , such as happiness. Thus, it causes people (staffs) lack motivated reasoning to unconsciously evaluate evidence in ways consistent with whose preferences. This type of bias can hinder a company's ability to learn from mistakes and to build successful strategies." However, Disney needed to implement knowledge management strategy to satisfy visitors demand after who entered .Disney demanded cleaners to repeat to remember any information to prepare to answer visitors' enquiries. It will train every cleaner memory to remember any information to be long term from short term memory successfully and every cleaner won't feel bore to do only cleaning job duty. When every one feel places are clean, who will concentrate on answering any visitors enquiries as the same time. Even, if they can give excellent service performance to serve visitors to let who to know how to go to any places in the short time. It is possible that visitors will appreciate whose service performance to let their manager to know, so that every cleaner will have chance to raise salary. Besides, waiting time and queues are daily problem for Disney theme park. Fast lines or priority queues appear as a solution of efficient queues for clients. Disney understood fast ticket line system affected visitor attendance numbers. Disney entertainment facilities long waits leaded to lower service evaluations and greater customer dissatisfaction. Efficient queue waiting time management can improve Disney visitor satisfaction and the willingness to recommend the service. Disney analysed of theme park visitor behaviour in relation to pay the higher ticket price to select to pay more for fast queuing line ticket than common queuing line ticket. In fact, Disney fast queuing line ticket system choice gave potential queues to any waiting clients . In general, Disney visitors don't like to wait long time in every entertainment facilities queuing line, who will feel a waste of time and waiting can lead to negative emotional response like frustration, impotence, tension or irritation .In fact, Disney amusement theme park needed visitors wait long queues and delays which were a frequent occurrence in every entertainment facilities line. Disney theme park as sets of rides, spectacles and leisure mechanisms are intended to entertainment and spark the imagination of clients, allowing visitors to escape their daily routing. In result, waiting is often a problematic issue that can influence Disney visitor experience and that can appear as one of the principal motives for complaining. As Disney visitor demand fluctuates constantly and demand patterns are often difficult to predict. It caused extra staff needed for the extra line. Finally, priority services such as fast line system facilities segmentation of its amusement park. When Disney offer the possibility of purchases a fast line, which are creating two different group. Disney visitors who are highly sensitive to waiting times are willing to pay to avoid or reduce lines or visitors that are highly sensitive to price that prefer to wait rather than to pay extra money. Also, Disney provides extensive training opportunity for participants through its own Disney university. The question of whether their training opportunity can lead the improve human resource activities. On the third hand problem, Disney are also worried that employees may leave it and join other competitor to serve their parks after training. Disney shows a trend of increasing depending on human capital other than physical capital. It thinks human capital is the knowledge, skills, ideas and commitment of its employees. It explains that investing in training and development is essential to its client service growth. In fact, Disney had owned enough entertainment facilities, restaurants, hotels, shopping centres within theme park, but its visitor numbers are increasing to need to be served satisfactorily. However, it needs to train cleaners, entertainment facilities service staffs, queuing service staffs, hotels, restaurants, shopping centres service staffs, instead of it's entertainment facilities attraction.

Disney observes that spending on training and development is typically regarded as consumption, instead of investment. On job training usually can't be replaced by formal education, therefore Disney chooses to make contribution on providing further training and development to employees. Disney paid salary for staff training, which included classroom, seminars, symposia or conferences; computer based training, on site training, book and periodicals reading, formal mentoring and informal mentoring program opportunities to meet its old staffs and new staffs both needs of motivate factors to achieve advancement , achievement, personal growth responsibility and achievement and recognition to raise its business performance effectively and efficiently. However, Disney's amount of training has a positive influence on intrinsic motivation of its employees. Job satisfaction, salary, working condition, its policies, administration, relationship with supervisors, peers and subordinates are Disney factors to influence it's human resource activities performance. Disney training contents include these functional area: Raising excellent service performance include that hotel food and beverage service delivery, shopping center, merchandise sale, restaurant service, entertainment facilities queuing waiting service, cleaning and enquiring how to go different locations in Disney, cashier service etc. They are very important to influence visitor numbers. Disney implementation of knowledge management solution to improve queuing waiting line process. The use of Disney front line service staffs as human capital combined with knowledge of customer preference has made the fast pass an innovation solution to enhance queuing in the Disney theme parks. Disney ability to capture customers in virtual queues when giving them a pleasurable waiting experience has made them a leader in knowledge management initiatives in the service industry. Disney's emphasis on human capital within their theme parks, combined with traditional queuing theory to create more pleasurable waiting environments. Hence, Disney showed the value of tacit employee knowledge integrated with traditional queuing theory to reduce loss of customer satisfaction to enhance, goodwill and profitability. Knowledge management expresses itself as human action in form of evaluation, attitudes, points of view, commitments, motivation etc. It seemed that Disney agreed that human capital (people, knowledge, ideas, creativity) maybe today's most valuable commodity.

Bibliography

Ansoff, H.I. (1987) Corporate Strategy. Penguin, London

Bahandin, G. & Guerganna, K.S. United States, (Jan. 2009).Strategic human resource management and global expansion lessons from the Euro Disney challenges in France. International business & economics research journal, vol. 8, no.1.

Barnard, Bruce: Business is booming in the world's biggest tourist market, March 1999, p.22, Journal of Commerce, Brucells.

Barnard, Bruce: Business is booming in the world's biggest tourist market, March 1999a, p.24, Journal of Commerce, Brucells.

Benesch, Dieter, 1989: " Theme parks in Florida-Eine Analyse von Angebot und Nachfrage sowie Regionalwirtschaftfliche Auswirkungen" , Master 's Thesis at the University of Economics and Business Administration, Vienna. AAdvisor: Prof. Dr. Karl Sinnhuber, Library.

Brennan, L. & Vecchi, A., (2011). The Business Of Space, The Next Frontier Of International Competition. Palgrave Macmillan Press: USA, New York.

Charles B. (2012) Curiosity Takes Us Back to Mars the
WHITE HOUSE Available at: Date Of Publication: 6 Aug.
https://www.whitehouse.gov/blog/2012/08/06/curiosity-takes-us-back-mars

Cope, R. R. Cope and H. Davis (2008). Disney's virtual Queues: A strategic opportunity to co-brand services ? Journal of Business & economics research, vol. 6 no10, 13-20.

Dickson, D., R. Ford and B. Laval (2005). Managing real and virtual waits in hospitality and service organizations. Corncell hotel and restaurant administration quarterly, vol. 45 no1, 52-68.

Dunn, J & A Neumsister (2002). Knowledge management in the Information age. E. business review, Fall , 37-45. Jounral of service, spring 2011, vol. 4, no1, De Grovte (2009).

Edinger Tourismberatung GmbH: Study: "Die Entwickling von Freizeitparks in Osterreich, 1998, for: Bundeministerium fur wirtschaftliche Angelegenheiten, wien" Innsbruck.

ERA (Economics Research Associates) 1998: " The Future Role of Theme parks in International Tourism" , Clive B. Jones & John Robinett, Los Angeles, p.5

ERA (Economics Research Associates) 1998a: " The Future Role of Theme parks in International Tourism" , Clive B. Jones & John Robinett, Los Angeles, p.13

Foden, harry G. 1996, " Destination attractions as an economic development generator", Economic Development Review, Fall 1996, 10., American Economic Development council

Friedmann, David:" Status Report of the Los Angeles County Economy", Vol.1, prepared for the "Los Angeles Board of Commerce, 1999.p.78

Futron Corporation (2009) Resource Centre. Available at:http://www.futron.com/resource_centre/resource_cemtre.htm.

Gartrell, R.B. (1994) Destination Marketing for Convention and Marketing Bureaus. Kendall/Hunt Publishing, Dubuque, Iowa

Harriet Griffey. (2010) The art of concentration, enhance focus, Reduce, stress and achieve move. Macmillan publishers ltd,Basinastoke and Oxford, London UK.

Hertzfeld, H.R. (2007) Globalization, Commercial Space And Space Power In the USA, Space Policy, Vol.32, no 4. November.

IAAPA: International Accociation of Amusement Parks and Attractions (http://www.iaapa.prg), " Theme Park Industry at-a-a glance" (Brochure), 1999, Atlanta, Georgia.

Kotler, P., Bowen, J. and Makens, J (2003) Marketing for Hospitality and Tourism. Prentice Hall ?Pearson Education, New Jersey

Kotler. P., Hamlin, M.A., Rein, I. and Haider, D.H (2002) Marketing Asian Places: attracting investment, industry, and tourism to cities, states & nations. John Wiley & Sons (Asia) Pte. Ltd., Singapore

Kotler, P., Haider, D.H. and Rein, I (1993) Place Marketing. Free Press, New York

Kyriazi, Gary, "Amusement Parks: A Pictorial History" Secaucus, NJ: Castle Booka, 1997.

Lundberg, Donals E. (ph.D.): " The Tourist Business", 1995, 5. Edition-Published by Van Nostrand Reinhold Company, New York.

Middleton, V.T.C. & Clarke, J. (2001) Marketing in Travel & Tourism. Butterworth Heinemann, Oxford

PKF consulting, 1997: " Study of the Projected Future Tax for: The City of Anadheim, the Anaheim Public Financing Authority, Nov. 13, Collections From Designated Sources to be Received by the city of Anaheim", 1997, prepared -1997.

Tarasenko, M.V. (1996) Evolution Of The Soviet Space Industry, Acta Astronautica, Vol. 38, no. 4-8, pp. 667-73.

The Economist 1997: "The Los Angeles economy: Bigger than South Korea", Feb, 4. 1997 page 25-26, London.

Wiig, k.(1993). Knowledge management foundations: Thinking About thinking. How people and organizations create, represent and use knowledge vol.1 , of knowledge management series schema press: Arlington, TX.

Yip, GS. (2003) Total Global Strategy II: Updated For The Internet And Service Era (Upper Saddle River, NT: Presentice-Hall).

Consumer psychology time

Ready-food meal short time cooking attractive factor

Ready-food meal can be attractive to change food consumers' long time cooking behavior. Because they can buy the ready cooking meal to heat to eat at home in short time. So, the short time cooking factor will influence many food buyers to choose to go to sumpermarkets to buy any taste of ready food to eat when they are busy to work ever day. I shall explain why an how shot time ready-food can change food consumer's choice to go to supermarkets to buy these any taste of ready-cooking food to replace the fresh food at food stores. Short time cooking factor is the major influence their food choice buying behavior.

Although, previously dismissed and a poor substitute for real cooking and ready meal sales have grown rapidly in recent years in many western developed countries, such as UK, France or Germany. But, Ready meal manufacturers ready to respond to a changing marketing environment. Due to one big change in recent year has been growing demand for ready prepared meals bought from a supermarket. An analysis of the reasons for the growth in the ready prepared meals markets indicates the effects of boards factors in the marketing environment on the size of a particular market. In fact, this food market is changing to drive the growth in the ready meals market, but there are differences in the food market potential between countries. The effect of change in the marketing environment on sales of ready meals, such as technology has played a big role in the growing take up of ready meals and new technologies have allowed companies to develop ready meals which preserve taste and texture, which still making them easy to use by the consumer. Furthermore, great advances in distribution management, in particular the use of information technology to control inventories, has allowed fresh, chilled ready meals to be effectively and efficiently distributed without the need for freezing or added preservatives. Ready meals particularly appeal to single householders, which individual family members tend to eat at different times, so family meals together remains stronger in many continental European countries than in the UK individual ready meals.

Young people have lost the ability to cook creatively, as cookery has been reduced in importance in the school, so young clients group will rise to buy ready meals from supermarket. Marketing can be seen as a system that must respond to environmental change. A food market can be defined as a meeting place for stakeholder (consumers) and sellers. Food market can be set up in a supermarket or restaurants. A food market consists of the individual's target taste, such as older group, family group, young group or business clients who are actual or potential caters of a restaurant meals or supermarket package of foods. Grocery stores (supermarkets) have an influence of meals (fast cooked food) outlets in low income urban areas, which has contributed to the income in access to healthy foods. An organization's marketing environment means the individuals, organizations, and forces external to the marketing management's ability to develop and maintain successful exchanges with its customers. The marketing environment to ready meal manufacturers had three levels.

Firstly, it includes the micro environment, it describes those elements that impinge directly on the ready meal manufacturers themselves, so the micro environment of ready meal manufacturers which include business clients who have direct contact, such as restaurants, supermarkets and individual clients who have direct contact. Otherwise, supermarket shoppers, restaurant clients and food supply competitors who have no direct contract to ready meal manufacturers, so who won't include in food market micro environment to ready meal manufacturers.

Secondly, it includes the macro environment, it describes things that are beyond the immediate environment but can nevertheless affect an organization, so the macro environment of ready meal manufacturers which include the export countries' economies forces, such as unemployment ratio, GDP; technological forces, such as the export countries' factories food productive technology; social/ cultural forces, such as the export countries' people taste acceptance; political/legal forces, such as the export countries' import food quota numbers.

Thirdly, it includes the internal environment, it describes ready meal manufacturers' employees and equipment and finance and functional responsibilities. Environment means everything outside influences the person, in contrast with individual or personal variables . The effects of change in the marketing environment on sales of ready meals can be analyzed by creating healthy food and eating environment changing factor and supermarket technological changing factor as below:

The ready meal manufacturers could not ignore threats to the natural ecological environment change Due to the food companies could have technology to manufacture good taste cooked ready meals to provide to supermarkets to sell. Thus, it might influence the consumers to decide whether restaurants or supermarkets or ready meals suppliers who could provide the most reasonable price and taste to satisfy whose eating needs every day. Thus, it caused the growing demand for ready prepared cooked meals bought from supermarkets. Due to it was possible that consumers felt to eat ready cooked meals in expensive restaurants or who did not like to buy foods to cook from food suppliers or who could not feel which could supply more good food taste and health food quality to compare supermarkets specially. Otherwise, although, supermarkets could provide cheaper ready cooked meals to satisfy who to feel good food taste and health food quality. Due to ready meal manufacturers had new techniques to develop ready meals which preserve taste and texture, which still making them easy to use to eat by the consumers. Furthermore, great advances in distribution management, in particular the use of information technology to control inventories, has allowed fresh , chilled ready meals to be effectively and efficiently distributed to supermarkets or restaurants without the need for freezing or added preservatives.

Creating healthy food and eating environments view describes an ecological framework for conceptualizing the many food environments and conditions that influence food choices, with an emphasis on current knowledge was been regarding the home, child care, school, work site, retail store and restaurant settings. The status of measurement and evaluation of nutrition environment and the need of action to improve health are highlighted in marketing environment. More processed and convenience foods are available in large portion sizes and which were supplied at relatively low prices at supermarkets. Parents are working larger hours, there are fewer family meals and more meals are eaten away from home. The school food environment is remarkably different. It seemed that it would be changed in the marketing environment on sales of ready cooked meals to supermarket more easily. Due to supermarkets' cooked meals should focus on selling high calorie and low nutrition foods are available in multiple venues throughout the school student client group target because it was possible that supermarkets could sell ready cooked ready meals prices were more cheaper to compare to restaurants or school canters' cooked meals provided prices.

The effects of change in the marketing environment on sales of ready meals which indicated that consumers chose prefer to buy ready cooked meals from supermarkets. It seemed that a restaurant market failure could be caused to arise. For example, there was poor information on the part of food (ready cooked meals) to provide to the restaurant about the foods that consumers in a location(place) would demand for a given price to compare to the supermarket sale prices. The restaurant would lose clients if which cooked the kind of meals to sell higher price to compare to the supermarket sale of the kind of cooked ready meals price possibly. Large size supermarkets could sell cheaper ready cooked meals to low income group clients. It could cause competition to constitute a market failure to small size supermarkets. If the small size supermarkets lacked good information on the true food (ready cooked meals) with concentrations to sell cheaper prices, then this ready cooked meal market failure was one potential reason why small size supermarkets did not locate to close to the large supermarkets. Due to supermarkets grew in size would influence clients' choice to buy the numbers of cooked foods (ready meals) products. Moreover, The advent of computerized logistics and inventory systems were integrated with the large size supermarkets themselves occurred between the 1980 years and 1990 years .

So large size supermarkets were reliance on their own distribution and cooked food (ready meals) inventory systems along with larger supermarket sizes to allow super center to change to sell ready cooked meals at lower prices. Supermarkets marketing can promote healthful eating by increasing availability, affordability or restricting / de-marketing unhealthy foods to sell cooked Food (ready meals) marketing strategy at supermarkets, including labelling, packaging, pricing and point of sale advertising. Consumers' cost saving efforts and income and ready cooked meals prices increasing or decreasing factors can drive the choice of supermarkets as well as cooked meal products use of coupons and loyalty cards bargain shopping is another factor to influence their choice. Private label or store (supermarket) brands are taking an increasing share of consumers shopping dollars as the importance of brands. Supermarket shoppers stated priorities are cooked food (ready meals) quality or taste and price and healthy cooked food (ready meals) choices.

However, supermarket shoppers' buying behaviors don't always reflect on favor healthful foods. Due to demand for locally grown cooked food is increasing. Anyway, restaurant meals are changed to supermarket to sell, which decide what kinds of meals to stock and how many of different kinds of meals to stock and how much variety of kinds of meals to offer to any one supermarket as well as supermarket shoppers prefer fewer options, provided that their preferred brand or cooked food (ready meals) products are available. The designs of supermarket ready cooked meal products and packaging to supermarket to sell is the focus of unusual colors or shape which can be used to increase interest and is specially pervasive among fun foods to compare to restaurant meals. Package design, including where text and images are placed, which can influences cooked foods (supermarket ready meals repurchasing again).The influence of design differs by the type of display consumer segments seek (convenience, information or images) and ready cooked meals package sizes have a relatively strong influence on consumption; larger ready cooked meals packages might increase per-use consumption ,but smaller packages might not improve self regulation and might not actually increase total consumption. In conclusion, I suggest that this ready meal manufacturers need to give more attention to be paid to food sellers, such as supermarkets' competitive differentiation and understanding the way in which customers attribute value to its ready meal products choice. Moreover, many consumers have become increasingly concerned about the health implication of the food they eat, so ready meal manufacturers will need to continue responding to such concerns. For example, who have responded with a range of low calorie meals, and addressed specific, sometimes transient, health fads, with respect to trans-fatty acids and omega 3 supplements of these cooked meal ingredients. Many consumers have also become concerned about the ecological environment and some supermarket suppliers, such as Marks and Spencer have incorporated sustainability agendas into their ready meals, for example by reducing packaging and sourcing supplies from sustainable sources. Thus, it caused ready meal manufacturers why who needed to give more attention to concern how supermarkets helped them to sell cooked ready meals in this foods market.

● Busy workers will be fast short time ready cooking meal consumer in supermarket

The macro environment, it describes things that are beyond the immediate environment but can nevertheless affect the organization. Such as the ready meal manufacturers in its macro environment, including the economic environment which can cause the manufacturers sell ready meal numbers whether which can sell more or less to different exported countries due to the exported countries' unemployment ratios, GDP and Government policies etc factors influence. Economic theory can help to explain why it can influence consumer behavior. In food sale market, it can include consumer behavior and demand side as well as retailer behavior and supply side two issues. Consumer behavior and demand side issue, such as the exported countries' consumer whose knowledge of the nutritional benefits of foods whether which prices were raised to choose to buy reasonably as well as retailer behavior and supply side issues, such as investing for developing a restaurant or supermarket in an underserved area whether the types of meals choices which are valued or which are not valued to buy to offer to clients from imports. On the other hand, economic environment factor, individual income can influence who chooses the type, quantity and quality of food that is purchased for a house holder and it also influenced the cooking and storage facilities available in a household to influence food choice.

On the other way, economic environment variation factor can also influence food access across areas. It is important to understand the economic conditions that may contribute to food deserts, that is the costs that food retail businesses face and the choice available to consumers who want to buy foods. Economic environment factor considers the consumer and demand factors, business and supply factors and the market conditions that interact to create differences in the food retail environment across areas and subpopulations. In general, high income meal client group can accept to choose to go to supermarkets or restaurants to spend than low income meal client group. The impact of the economic environment on sales of ready meals is such as an individual get richer, who can afford to buy ready prepared foods, rather than spend time and effort to prepare to cook them at home. It seemed that low income consumers were decreasing to eat meals at expensive restaurant to the alternative of relatively cheap ready prepared meals at home.

Research could also consider how consumer knowledge and preferences and the time cost tradeoffs affect consumer decisions of which foods to eat and whether to make or to buy prepared foods from supermarkets or to eat at restaurant meals . Travel costs and time costs of acquiring foods as well as the time costs of preparing foods (meals) are also likely to affect demand for particular foods. Research on price variation at the local level and demand models could also be used to help determine which factors contribute to differences in access to food retailers. Price is also major determinant of food (meal) demand. The higher, the price of a food(meal), the lower the meal quantity demanded. On the other hand, the higher the price of a substitute food (meal), the higher demand will be for that food (meal) item. Given the budget constraints of low income consumers and the price of some specific foods (meals), low income consumers may substitute higher priced foods (meals) with lower priced foods(e.g. hamburger for steak or canned fruits for fresh fruits). Considering restaurants foods purchasing choice, such as economies of scale, which is when the costs of operating a restaurant decreases as restaurant size increases and economies of scope, which is when the costs decrease as more meals variety increases, suggests that larger restaurants that offer greater variety can offer lower meal prices. Both factors may account for the ability of larger restaurants to survive more easily than smaller restaurants. Considering supermarkets foods purchasing choice, it is possible that food retailers (supermarkets) actually have some market power, especially in setting where there are few competitors to close. It would have an incentive to increase food (ready meal) price and restrict foods(ready meals) supply quantities to increase profit. Supply side conditions, such as economies of scale, it could lead to (ready meal) food retailers (supermarkets) to have more market power, if it was not close between supermarkets. Individual behavior to make healthy choices can occur only in a supportive economic environment with accessible and affordable healthy food choices. Hence, food environment and sale strategies is needed to consider to adopt the exported countries' economic change.

Food marketing client target groups can include home parents, students and working people groups mainly and marketing and economic environment factors would cause food choices and
these factors impact health and nutrition and the focus on the connections between people and their environments.
In conclusion, macro level economic environmental factors play a more

indirect role but have a substantial and powerful effect on what people eat. Macro level factors operate within the larger society, include food marketing, social norms, food production and distribution systems, agriculture policies and economic price structures as well as social environmental to influence within the home, such as model of healthful dietary intake by parents feeding style, frequent family meals may promote healthful food consumption among children.

● Short time fast ready cooking meals will be Hong Kong busy food consumers market

Hong Kong people can choose to go to restaurants to eat or go to supermarkets to buy foods to cook to eat. Although, ready meal manufacturers had increased the sale numbersof the ready prepared meals in many western countries in recent years. However, there still had any factors to limit it's sale numbers to Hong Kong market over the next five years, so it needed to aware of what was changing in Hong Kong food market environment and appreciated how change in this Hong Kong food environment to lead to change patterns of eating cooked ready meals demand to attempt to win its similar food competitors in Hong Kong market next five years. Hong Kong food environment related to Hong Kong people eating behaviors, include social environments and physical environments and macro level environment.

The cooked meal quality and quantity of available can influence food numbers to produce meal to supply to Hong Kong food market. Hence, Hong Kong natural climatic change can influence the overseas food supply numbers to be imported to cause meals prices to go up or go down. If next five years, Hong Kong climate was good to grow plants and feed animals e.g. pigs and cows etc. meats. The restaurant meals or supermarket meals sale prices can be cheaper due to farmers who have much foods and vegetables to supply , so who can sell cheaper price to these restaurants or supermarkets to cause whose production cost to be decreased next five years in my country. Hence, ready meals prices could not sell more higher than Hong Kong meals prices. Hong Kong people eating behaviors are often changed over a lifetime. In general, Hong Kong people want to eat to satisfy physical hunger and psychological desires and yet want to be healthy, which may enquire adopting eating patterns that conflict with these desires. My country people make decisions about food several times a day: when to eat, what to eat, with where to eat and how much per meal prices and how much per meal numbers .

In general, Hong Kong people like to eat Chinese foods , but who also like to go to restaurants to eat or supermarkets to buy western foods, such as liking of specific tastes are important influences. However, these can be modified by experience with food from various intrapersonal and interpersonal factors to influence Hong Kong people to choose to buy uncooked or cooked meals from Hong Kong supermarkets. The next five year, food retailer behavior and supply factors of food access might affect overseas sales of ready meals numbers imported to my country. In general, supply is driven by the costs of input foods. The land, materials, machines and labor costs are needed to build and operate a restaurant or supermarkets. If these costs are increased to these food suppliers in my county next five years, overseas food demand shall be caused to be decreased if Hong Kong economy had changed to be worse and the new restaurants and supermarkets which costs were changed to be higher to much as well as Hong Kong unemployment was caused to be raised and many people lost jobs to have efforts to go to supermarkets to buy higher prices ready meals or go to restaurants to eat higher price ready meals.

My country's social environment and physical environment which also might affect sales of ready meals numbers next five years. Social environment includes interactions, with family, friends, peers and others in the community to impact food choices through mechanisms as well as physical environment includes the different places where people eat or buy food, such as whether the supermarkets or restaurants locations which are close to the buyers, e.g. schools, offices, houses. Hence, food suppliers' locations choice can influence who (target client groups) choose to buy more or less ready meals numbers. Foods prepared at home factor there may be relatively greater time costs than those to buy cooked foods(ready meals) from supermarkets or takeout foods. Hong Kong consumers may value the convenience of a fast food or takeout cooked meal more because it doesn't require spending much time to prepare to cook at home. Hence, Hong Kong people whose taste is for different kind of cooked foods (ready meals) and who feel the food suppliers' locations whether are convenient and Hong Kong economy whether is better or worse to cause unemployment numbers next five years, these factors can affect sales of imported ready cooked or uncooked meal numbers to my country Hong Kong next five year.

CHAPTER TEN

Time pressure influences traveller behavior

I shall explain how time pressure influences airport passengers consumption behavior and travel agents choice behavior. Nowadays, travellers enjoy to go to different countries to travel. In consumer psychological view, instead of the travelling agents' travelling e-ticket cheap and fast seats online booking service or walk in travelling travel agents travelling paper ticket purchase or attractive trip arrangement service to attract travelling consumers' choice.

In any countries, whether attractive airport appearance design, airport convenient public transportaton tools service, e.g. enough airport bus, taxi, train, tram , underground train , ferry etc. number supplying , which can let any foreign travellers find and choose any kinds of public transportaton tools to catch to arrive destinations when they arrive any countries' airports easily, different kinds of varoety of attractive product shops or food courts/ shops which can let airport passengers to sit down and choose any kinds of food to eat or they can choose any books, magazines, or stationerys or cigarettes, wine, toys , electronic products, e.g. desktop, laptop computers etc. products to consume for reading or using need in the airport's any restaurants or ships conveniently.

All these airports' intangible or tangible factors whether they can influence consumers' shopping desires in airports, even whether these both factors can attract or persuade many travellers prefer to choose to go to the country to travel and increase the country's travellers number. Concerning these two questions, my readers can earn more useful opinions to analyse whether any country's airport's image will have relationship to influence travellers' tourism choice and tourism consumption choice behavior , due to the country's airport's facility management , service, appearance design

, convenient transportation, safety etc. important factors influence in order to assist to develop the country's tourism industry success in possible.

Nowadays, global travelling entertainment activities are popular. Some travellers like domestic travelling or some travellers like to catc airplanes to go to other countries travel. In consumer behavioral view point, when the consumer discovers the product's price is higher than the another product's price. Then, he/she will usually to choose to buy the cheaper product, such as travel agent travelling entertainment activities arrangement service case, whether the travelling provider charges higher travelling entertainment activities arrangement service fee to compare the another similar travelling entertainment activities arrangement service provider. Does this travelling entertainment activities similar fee comparison factor influence any travellers choose to find the cheaper travelling entertainment activities arrangement provider? If travelling entertainment activities arrangement price is not the main factor to influence traveller individual choice. What other factors can influence traveller individual travelling entertainment activities arrangement choice? I shall explain what the other factors are influcenced traveller individual travelling entertainment arrangement choice.

The factors include that the cultural distance on satisfaction and travel intention factor, the lifestyle concept in travel behavioral factor, the business travellers motivation behavioral factor, the impacts of peer-to-peer accommodation use on travel patterns factor, factors influence local tourists decision-making be on choosing a destination factor, transportation, shopping centers, travelling destination facilities supplying factor, social media travelling networking sites promotion factor, traveller's travelling experience psychological factor, travelling service for disabled people's travelling need factor, green travel entertainment service for environment protection travelling environment need factor the impact of travel blogging on the tourist, traveller individual vacation destination choice factor, economic impact to the traveller individual sudden changing factor.

Therefore, it brings these questions: How any why traveller individual travelling choice won't be influenced by travelling entertainment service price only? Does it mean the travelling entertainment service providers will not reduce their traveller number when they can respect or consider above factors to avoid to bring negative influence to traveller consumers, but they still change higher travelling entertainment arrangement service fee to them?

This final part , such as travel entertainment industry, nowadays global travelling entertainment activities are popular, some travellers like domestic travelling or some travellers like to catch airplanes to go to other countries travel. In consumer behavioral view point, when the consumer discovers the product's price is higher than the another product's price. Then, he/she will usually to choose to buy the cheaper product, such as travel agent travelling entertainment activities arrangement service case, whether the travelling provider charges higher travelling entertainment activities arrangement service fee to compare the another similar travelling entertainment activities arrangement service provider. Does this travelling entertainment activities similar fee comparison factor influence any travellers choose to find the cheaper travelling entertainment activities arrangement provider? If travelling entertainment activities arrangement price is not the main factor to influence traveller individual choice. What other factors can influence traveller individual travelling entertainment activities arrangement choice? I shall explain what the other factors are influenced traveller individual travelling entertainment arrangement choice.

The factors include that the cultural distance on satisfaction and travel intention factor, the lifestyle concept in travel behavioral factor, the business travellers motivation behavioral factor, the impacts of peer-to-peer accommodation use on travel patterns factor, factors influence local tourists decision-making be on choosing a destination factor, transportation, shopping centers, travelling destination facilities supplying factor, social media travelling networking sites promotion factor, traveller's travelling experience psychological factor, travelling service for disabled people's travelling need factor, green travel entertainment service for environment protection travelling environment need factor the impact of travel blogging on the tourist, traveller individual vacation destination choice factor, economic impact to the traveller individual sudden changing factor.

Therefore, it brings these questions: How any why traveller individual travelling choice won't be influenced by travelling entertainment service price only? Does it mean the travelling entertainment service providers will not reduce their traveller number when they can respect or consider above factors to avoid to bring negative influence to traveller consumers, but they still change higher travelling entertainment arrangement service fee to them? In my this part, I shall explain above factors how to influence traveller individual behavior to let readers can predict traveller individual behavior more accurately.

● Time pressure influences airport actual functionality and passengers consumption behavior

Instead of airport is one arrical and leaving terminal station place main function for any travelling passengers after the airplances had landed on the country airport's subway. I feel that airport has also another main functions. It can help the country to attract more travellers to choose to go to the country to travel as well as it can persuade them to raise consumption desire in their whole journeys after they leave the travelling country's airport if they feel the country airport's service performance can satisfy their short time staying need. I shall explain why any countries' airports can influence travellers' travelling destinations and travelling shopping choices to be increased or decreased.

The future airport will be the assistance role to assist tourim industry development. The factors include, for example, safety and terrorism control, when the travellers feel the country's airport is safe to stay when they catch air planes to arrive the coutry first time. Then, the country's airport can build safe image to let them to feel the country is safe to travel indirectly, traditional cirport service providers will need to seek new service way to deliver value, such as subscription based service models can let travellers to feel the country's airport can provide one comfortable and enjoyable short term travelling staying environment in the country's airport. Then, they bring pleasant emotion to prepare their journey trip after they leave the airport in the foreign country.

So, if the country's airport can let the travellers feel safe and comfortable , then it can bring new exciting and enjoyable feeling to the country's image. Because airport will be any travellers' first time arrival place after they catch airplanes to arrive another country. So, positive or negative airport's image will influence travellers how they feel whether the country , it is worth to choose to travel indirectly. However, airports need have good facilities to satisfy any related airplane service employees or any airport food or product businesses need, instead of travellers' need. For example, it needs have good allocation of terminals and access to facilities , they will be managed and regularly reviewed and regarded their good facility availability , capacity constraints and the best use of available facilities to satisfy any food or product sale shops' sale need and airport passengers' purchase need both in airports or airplane pilots, airplace service employees, irport security employees' comfortable working environment need.

However, airport inside and outside also needs to be arranged enough parking space facilities to let any aircraft parked or stored at the airport from the place where it is parked or stored in order to let any vehicles to be parked in airports or ouside airports easily and conveniently. When any sudden emergency matters occurred, the aircraft subjects to unforeseen operational delays , it should need to contact airport operations control centre to indicate when the expected time of arrival and departure is, there is no need to request a new slot in cases of unforeseen operational delays where the operation will take place within 24 hours of the agreed slot time. For example, of unforeseen operational delays include aircraft technical issues or weather conditions that could not have been planned for. Hence, operationally delayed aircraft must utilise slots in the same manner as originally agreed. If any change to the original slot agreement is required, e.g. a slot must be requested immediately. Moreover, when aircraft subjects to non-operational delays must request new slots immediately, following the correct process in those conditions of use, an example, of a non-operational delay may include delay caused by late running passengers or poor schedule planning. Hence, airport needs have good facilities and communication system to coordinate to any departments to avoid aircraft unforeseen delays to cause airport passengers feel nervous and brings negative and poor emotion to the airport's service performance.

On airport baggage handling function aspect, airport operators must comply with the baggage policy made available to all operators with the airline business management team. For example, where a flight destination or carrier is identified as being at significant or high risk, the operator will pay a charge as notified by management, equating to the cost of any policing cost additional to the services normally provided at the airport for carriers or destinations at lower levels of risk. In fact, airport baggage management needs be checked and delivered in order to help any airplanes' passengers to transport their baggages to follow their airplanes to be delivered to their same destinations when their airplanes are flying with the passengers and whom baggages to arrive the same country's airport at the same time absolutely. So, barrage management operators need submit or demand and in agreed format the already fleets absolutely, such as fleet detail to report these data to include aircraft type and registration, number of seats maximum take off weight kilogrammes of each aircraft owned or operated by the operator, in order to avoid any passengers' luggages wrong delivery occurrence in possible.

Hence, any airports must need to consider above basic passenger service operation in order to avoid any accident occurrences to bring poor airport service attitude feeling. If airport management expected that they have good service performance to satisfy travellers' short term staying needs in themselve countries' airport.

● How airport strategies solve passengers

feeling time pressure challenge

Any countries' airports expect to increase passenger movements, they must have effective strategies to carry on reviewing any errors and improve performance effectively. For instance, how to keep cost effective measures to lower operating costs and keep good performance on quality, such as for maintenance and cleaning airport cost reducing measures to introduce variable, performance -based elements to encourage productivity gains, how to manage and implement new technological systems to improve information flow and work processes within the country's airport, e.g. airport e-immigration system can allows to receive real-time alerts on any airport building faults. It can reduce airport reliance on manpower in these areas, thus reaulting in better productivity and cost savings for long term airport expenditure. So, high technological strategy system is needed to implement to any country's airport in order to facilitate the handling of more aircraft movements to optimise aircraft handling on runways. Their benefits include reduction of departure flights separation times, reconfiguration of flight routes, and improvements in runway inspection processes.

These new measures can bring effective in improving any country's airport's runway efficiency, developing new infrastructure including the extension of the taxiway, roadway and power supply networks. It aims to satisfy travellers' convenient transportation needs when they arrive any countries' airports and prepare to find suitable transportaton tools to arrive their destinations more easily (airport transportation roadway, taxiway building network strategy).

Hence, any countries' airports need have good strategy to manage a wide range of activities and risks, which are broadly classified into strategic , financial operational, regulatory and investment. Any countries' airports also need to seek how to reduce the occurrence of risks and to minimum potential adverse impact as much as possible, uch as airport risk management strategy. Because when the country has many people are living and they need often to catch airplanes to leave their countries to travel as well as there are many foreign travellers choose to travel the country. Then, the country's airport must need to expand size and raise good facilities, e.g. more automated immigration gantries are needed to be installed, taxi waiting areas are also needed to be explanded with additional taxi bays constructed to accommodate the higher number of arriving passengers , even increasing airplane subways number to satisfy many airplanes need to fly away from the country's airport or coming airplances fly to the country's airport's landing on runway needs often.

So, airplane subways number expanding strategy and cutomated immigration gate fast checking system is needed when the country has many travellers choose to go to the country travel and/or many local people need to leave themselves countries to travel. For instance, departure and arrival immigration control as well as pre-boarding security screening will be controlled for more efficient deployment of manpower and equipment. Moreover, in the line will the trend of self-service options of airports arrived the world, provisions will be made to have more kioslls for self check in,self-bag -tagging and self bad-drops. The increasing use of these options will help airlines and ground handling agents reduce processing times and staffing requirement. For example, a fully automated to reduce reliance on scare manpower baggage check in and check out system, the baggage handling system will also be equipped with ergonomic lifting aids to enable heavy and odd-sized bags to be handled with ease, even by older workers.

Then, the country's airport must need to increase subways number and immigration fast checking service facility to avoid handling passengers crowd queueing problem often occurs every day. When any airports often let passengers feel time pressure to queue to spend long time to wait immigration checks and leave the airport. It will bring their negative emotion feeling to the country's airport. Then, it is possible to influence they choose to go to the country to repeat travel again. Hence, the country's different airport strategies are needed when the country has increasing travellers number trend as soon as possible.

Another strategy concerns airport emergency service on safe aspect. Any countries' airports need have a highly trained specialist wait that is positioned to provid fast action rescue and fire protection for passengers' life safety ,e .g. aircraft rescue and fire fighting vehicles are needed airport. An incident command and control simulator which provides realistic and interactive simulations of emergency scenarios for the purpose of any sudden accident occurrences in any countries' airports.

So, any countries' airports need to develop an internal digital system to ease labour-intensive work processes like fire safety inspection, incident reporting, logistic management and recording of its personal fitness results, with the new safe system , data entry is needed mobile enabled with the use tablet computers. For example, the airport safe unit can continue to enhance its emergency preparedness and rescue capabilities with the successful staging of two drills, simulated aircraft crashes on land and at sea, as well as any exercises validated crisis contingency plans are recommended to earn strong capability in coordinating rescue efforts involving both the airport community and mutual aid agencies in order to carry on rescuing passengers and airport pilots and service attendants whom life safe service when air planes are crashed on land and at sea.

Another strategy is now aviation facilities strategy, it can support fly, cruise and fly-coach initatives, important options to a rising number of interm travellers, if it can be implemented successfully. It can bring enhancement measures benefits, includes the reduction of departure flight separation times, reconfiguring of flight routes and implementation of aircraft speed control for increased runway use efficiency.

Hence, one successful airport operation , the airport management needs to know how to implement the traveller check out or check in service functions when they arrive the airport or leave the airport and to satisfy its passengers' short term terminal station staying or transfering another airplane's flying need as well as it also needs to know how to implement its different strategies to improve its service performance and to let passengers have more confidence to the country's airport service operators' behavior and they also feel safe when they are staying the country's airport. Hence, any travellers' short term staying feeling in the country's airport , whether the country's airport can bring either positive or negative emotion , which will influence they choose to go to the country to travel again in possible. Hence, airport management can not neglect how to improve airport service performance to satisfy any first time or more time airport visitors' short term staying need.

● Long time airport staying bring passengers
positive consumption emotion

It is an interesting question: Can the country's airport service performance influence passengers consumption desire? Nowadays, travelling is a kind of popular entertainment whn working people have holidays, retired people have more savings and students need to go to holiday to feel rest time after they had hard to study. They will choose go to other countries to travel. So, " freguent travelling times" which will increase to any travelling consumers. If the traveller often chooses to go to the country to travel, he must need to permit to enter the country from its airport immigration. If his every visiting time to the country's airport, he feels the country's airports' staffs services are poor performance and he feels that they are not polite or rude attitude to treat him when he needs to check out or check in from the country's airport immigraton gates, even he feels difficult to enquire any airport service staffs, either he feels difficult to find them or they need to spend long time to let him to queue to wait enquiry, even he also needs to spend long time to queue to wait check in or check out in airport immigration gates when he arrives the country's airport or he leaves the country's airport.

All of these negative airport staffs' service attitudes and poor service behavioral feeling, they will cause the frequent traveller doubts whether the country is a worthy travelling place and it is possible to led his negative consumption desire in the country's airport. Then, all of these negative emotion will influence the frequent traveller reduces consumption in the country's airport , even wothut any consumption in the country's airport, when he visits the country to travel every time. So , it seems that airport's service performance will influence travellers carry on more or less consumption in the country's airport. Then, it will influence all the country's airport related retail and restaurant businesses' sales to be reduced indirectly in the country's airport.

Instead of airport service performance intangible factor aspect, the airport's clean, airport itself appearance attractive design, large size and shops and restaurants' suitable locations and internal environment design etc. these tangible factors will also influence travellers' consumption desires in the country's airport. For example, in one special day, e.g. Olympic Games day, the Olympic Games country's airport may complete in record time and its airport can successfully handle a estimate record 85,000 minimum departing passengers a day during the Olympic Games period, twice the number on normal days. Travellers and media will describe the Olympic Games country's airport retail shops and restaurants consumption experience as seamless, magical and unforgettale airport staying experience, if the Olympic games country's airport can provide an excellent service performance on the Olympic games period. Then, it will influence the increasing sale amount in the Olympic Games country airport retail stores and restaurants during period. So , when the country is experiencing special day, such as "Olympic Games " is chosen to carry on competition in the country. Then, in this Olympic Games period, it will attract many travellers to choose to go to this country to travel, due to they have interest to watch Olympic Games competition in this country. This country's airport will represent this country's image. If it 's airport service staffs can provide excellent service to let any one of travellers to feel when they are staying in this country's airport short time and this country's airport itself appearance and design can also be changed more attractive and beautiful and the airport's retail stores and restaurants also design more attractive and beautiful. Then, the travellers' consumption desires will be possible to raise , when they visit this country's airport in first time in this Olympic Games travelling period.

● Global air transport network attractive strategy

In the future, if the country has a strong and affordable global air transport network, it will bring more advantages. Due to many travellers expect to catch air planes which can fly to another country in short time , it can reduce accidents occurrence chance on sky or on sea. So, short time flying can be more attract to compare long time flying. So, it explains that why many travellers prefer to choose one way flying more than transfering another /other air plane(s) flying. Although, they need to pay more air ticket fee. So, if the country's airport can have more subways number and large subways areas to let many arrival air planes and leaving air planes need to fly from land or fly to land in the country's airport frequently. Then, the travellers can buy any air tickets to book same day or next day or later day flught time to fly to any country to travel more easily, when the country's airport has large area size and many subways to let many airplanes can stay in its aircraft subways in same time. Then, the country's airport flight frequency will increase , it means that there are many travellers can catch airplances to fly to other countries in any time very easily from themseleves country's airport. It is time-sensitive feeling to let the country's travellers, they can feel to fly to other countries to travel in short day. They do not need delay to fly to any countries, when the flight airline is either full seat or the time can not permit any air places land on the country's subways.

So, none delaying time sensitive travelling frequent flught model will be one attractive flight flying method to influence the country's travellers choose to frequent travelling behavior. Because they do not change their travelling day, due to airplanes have no enough seats supply or the country's airport has no enough land subways to let any airplanes to stay to cause delaying their flight travelling booking seat day expectly.

So, airport is similar to airline to need to use different customer relationship management to attract returning travelling customers . It brings this question: What are the most attractive motivation factors in airport travel market?

I believe that factors may include airport loyalty, various flight time arrangement distribution channel, passenger check in or check out, laggage safe delivery, airpor security service. Moreover, flight schedules are also a main factor influences the travellers' final travelling country choice decision among different travelling countries. However, if the country's airport can build good loyalty image when passengers are staying in the country's airport in short time, it can show a more attractive motivator to increase travellers' consumption desires when they are staying in the country's airport in short time.

Hence, airport 's loyalty seems have relationship to influence travellers' consumption behavior when they are staying in the country's airport. For example, when the different countries' travellers feel enjoyable and happy to stay in the country's airport longer time. Then, their airport long time staying behavior will raise their consumption desire and chance to find any right restaurant to eat food or drink or find any right retail shop to buy right products in airport. Hence , when the country's airport can buil loyal customers relationship. Then, it will bring the advantages or benefits to the airport's any retail shops or restaurants on sale growth aspect, such as : their retention rates will go up easier, their customer referrals will go up easier, the country airport retail shopd and restaurants travelling customers whom spending rates will go up easier, the country airport retail shops and restaurants customers will be loss price sensitive, the costs of retail and restaurant servicing then will go down easier. Hence, if the country's airport customer service performance can maximize travellers' loyalty. It will influence travellers to feel the country airport's retail shops and restaurants have more loyalty to compare other countries airports' retail shops and restaurants loyalty.

So, it implies that any any country airport's loyalty will have relationship to influence its travellers how they feel the country airport's retail shops and restaurants' loyalty. Due to loyalty is intangible and it is obly feeling. So, when the travellers have positive emotion and wheh they are staying in the country's airport long time. Then, they will have positive emotion to spend more time to walk around in the country's airport as well as when they are passing any airport's retail shops or restaurents. Their pleasant emotion may encourage their consumption behaviors to have interest to find any right restaurant to eat food or drink or find any right retail shop to buy any right product in the country's airport in preference easily. Because they had been accepted to spend long time to stay in the country's airport, when they feel interest and surprise to visit the country airport when they arrive. Moreover , the long airport staying time will increase their purchase chance to any the country's airport's retail stores or restaurants in the country 's airport in first time visiting.

● How to satisfy customer expectation
for long time staying passenger service at airport
When one country's airport can satisfy passengers expectation to accept its service demand, then profitability and passenger number will be influenced to increase. So, airport management needs to focus on how to satisfy any passenger individual need or expectation when he/she needs to stay in whose country's airport for wait to either transferinf another airplance need to carrying on check in or check out in the country's airport immigration gate need in short time.

However, because if the country's airport service can let its passengers feel happy , then they will be super spenders to spend airport staying longer time to consume or entertain in the country's airport. Moreover, it will bring any the country airport's retail shops or restaurante to earn more sale growth indirectly. So, any country airports need to consider how to bring excellent customer services for any passenger individual need in airport. Because its service behavior or performance will have indirect relationship to impact the county airport's any businesses and itself any parking , entertaining services income in airport.

" The concept of managing airport customer expectation on passenger service quality" will be any country airport's main aim. Basically, airport passengers' perception concern how the airport service staffs' service attitudes or performances influence how they feel either negative emotion, such as anger, dissatisfaction, irritation, neutrality or positive emotion, such as happy, satisfaction, pleasure, delight. So, when the airport passenger individual perception is better , then his expected to the country airport individual service staff level will be at the highest level, but if his service expectation is less than his expectation standard, then the airport passenger will dissatisfy with the lowest satisfaction level to be influenced the country airport's other any one service staff by the one airport service staff whose poor performance. Because any one of the country airport's service staff , every one will influence the country airport's image. Of every one has excellent service performance, then, it will let many different counties' passengers feel sympathetic emotion from their every one's behavior. Otherwise, if every one has or most service staffs have poor or not considerate ot not sympathetic service attitude to be let them to feel, then any one of them will let many itself airport's countries' passengers feel the country airport's image is poor. They won't like to spend long time to stay in the country airport, even their short time airport staying behaviors will influence the country airport's any retail shops or restaurants businesses sale growth to be reduced from their short staying time influence.

In general, airport service staffs need to spend some time to answer any passengers' enquiries. So, how they answer their enquiries will influence how their achievement in order to raise the country airport's passengers satisfactions. It may lead a rise in different countries'passengers' loyalty and retention, therefore the country airport can increase many different countries passengers number when the repeating airport visitors , they prefer to choose to go to the country to travel again , due to its airport is attractive reason in possible.

So, any country airport management ought have a policy from how the airport established desirable standard performance, measure it against actual performance to action taken once and revise any unachieved acceptable service level to the acceptable excellent passenger service performance in the country airport. For example, any country airport needs to manage and identify the target passenger segmenation target groups and to make bettwe understand the key elements that have the greatest impact on meeting every different target passenger segmentation group individual expectations and needs from their services in themselves country airport. So, any country airport will have relationship to any one of airline, as well as any one airline will have direct relationship to every passenger when he/ she stays in the country airport in short time.

However, instead of restaurants and retail shops; sale relationship will be influenced by the country airport's service performance, airport management also bring more empahsis on non-aeronautical (non related airlined and retail business) revenues, such as shops rents, concessions, car parking service income, consultancy and property developed diversified service incomes. So, airports need to focus directly to enterainment travelling airlines' passengers, meeters, and greeters, business-travelling passengers , users of general aviation services and transfer air plane short time staying visitors, or lone time staying visitors, e.g. the passengers need to live airport hotel for on night or more than one night sleeping before they catch the airplane on the day. So, all these different target passenger segmentations will have different service needs in any country airports.

However, airport passengers' behaviors and expectations of the airport experience depend highly on the types of traveller, they include: demographic characteristics, (i.e. gender, age group, income, sex, occupation) , purpose of trip (i.e. leisure, business), and their circumstances. In general , the passenger can be divided into different group, such as arriving, departing and transfer with different expectation and need, in the way they will be using the airport services and facilities different need and will also influence the behavior of individuals when in the commercial area. For example, passengers who are departing and arriving will require all airport facilities including: car rental, rail, buses access, pre-booking taxi service, check in or check out service, bad processing and security check and vertical and horizontal moving in passenger terminals. Otherwise, transfer passengers will have a short waiting time in airport and their needs will be likely different from those of origin and destination passengers. Some of the transit passengers will need to spend one hour, even more than four hours or half day in the airport. By providing airport facilities that can accommodate their needs, such as a place to lie down and take a short sleep time, free shower, free email public service will mostly give than an enjoyable airport experience. Evem some handicapped people or old people who feel difficult to walk in the airport corridor. Then , the airport will need to arrange the auto -wheel chairs and auto airport vehicle facilities to let service staffs to provide electronic auto wheel chairs to let them to sit down or drive the auto airport vehicle to sit down with them to go to their destination in the airport's any places immediately. For passengers travelling with families may want children play areas, where kids can have a great time when waiting to board the aircraft. They also want the availability of rooms of families travelling with badies equipped with changing facilities, baby crib, microwaved and hot water need. When passengers are on business trip, may want a lounge, with all the business, facilities that they can feel free to use, such as free internet access and other services , such as fax, scan and photocopy machine. Hence, any airport managements need to develop the strategic customer facilities providing service in order to improve the design and delivery of all the facilities and services need by understanding expectation of each passenger segmentation group in their airport staying time.

Finally , in airport unique design aspect, our global airports will need have different unique design to let any travellers to feel that the country's airport can have its unique design to let themm to feel the country airport has itself own airport culture or entertainment features to attract they observe its appearance in order to achieve the increase more travelling visitors number when they feel enjoy to stay in the country airport longer time before they leave the airport. I shall indicate different countries' airports how they will perform themselves different airport cultures and unique design as below:

For China and Hong Kong Chinese airport design example, their airports need have Chinese cultural feeling to let Western travellers to feel their airports' designs and cultures are different to any Western countries' other cultures. So, China anf Hong Kong airports' designs can increase many old big size building photos number in their airports to let foreign visitors can walk on the long glass walkway corridor , when they enter walkway coddidor to walk through different 100 more airplane leaving and arriving gates number and the ground floor is built from heavy glass material. So , any one foreign traveller need to walk through on the long glass walkway corridor to pass any one gates to arrive his/her airplane leaving and arriving gate location and catch airplance to fly. Also, the glass walkway ground floor can let them to see the airport's vehicles and airplanes and people and trees outside environment clearly when they are walking on the airports' all glass material manual made ground floor. It will let foreign travellers feel China and Hong Kong airports building designs are different to the foreign countries' themselves airports' designs as well as Hong Kong and China airports' old building photos will let all leaving passengers feel difficult to forget their old building historical photos and they will know hoe their architectural skills are developed to imprved to build nowadays unqiue desing method from traditional building design method in Hong Kong and China airports. Otherwise, for US, Uk etc. foreign countries their airports designs can increase underground floor fish pool architectural design outside to their airports in order to let any passengers feel that they can see many different kinds of various fishes are swimming. So, their outside large fish pool can let them to feel surprise when they are staying in their any airports, e.g. one beautiful large size fish pool, it can be built to close to their airports and the fish pool can have various kinds of big and small fishes swim in the pool to let passssngers to see, or their airports can appear suddenly and unexpected of a gaping hole in the airport's outside ground, known as a sinkhole. Sometimes, the airport's outside sinkhole will fill up with fresh water to become deep , shaped manual made sinkhole to let passengers to feel they need to enter to the sinkhole and then they can enter the airport. So, the outside large size sinkhole will attract many passengers to stat to observe how the fresh water is entering to the sinkhole interestingly. Then, they will feel surprise when they need to pass though the sinkhole , then they can enter the airport.

In conclusion, attractive airport architectural design will let any passengers can not forget that they had ever visit the country to travel in their travelling experience as well as they can be influenced to like to stay longer time in the country airport by the airport's attractive design and environment influence. The most important influnece, it can influence airport related business income when they like to stay longer time in the airport.

● Long time cultural distance factor on satisfaction respects travel intention

Every country cultural difference is different. How and why cultural difference has a real impact on tourist satisfaction and it can also influence to repeat travel. Is cultural tourism one major factor to influence tourist to repeat travelling intention or choice to the country in international tourism choice market? For example, China and India have similar culture. Their cultural difference is not much, e.g. eating cultural habit is similar , entertainment cultural habit is similar. These both countries people do not want to spend much money in eating and entertainment both aspects. Hence, these two countries people do not consider how to consume to enjoy entertainment and eat expensive food. Hence, it is based on cultural similar reason. These both countries tourists will prefer to choose to repeat travelling either China or India. When the Indian tourists had chosen to go to China to travel in the first time. Then, the Indian tourists will choose to go to China to travel in second time again. Also, the Indian tourists had chosen to go to China to travel in first time. Then, the Chinese tourists will choose to go to India to travel in second time again.

What factors influence China and India tourists respect to travel between these both countries. The factors will include cheap air ticket price, cheap hotel living price , less economic cost factor. However, I believe the similar cultural factor will be the major factor to influence many Chinese and Indian tourist prefer to choose to repeat travelling between these both countries.

As my indication to these both countries people have similar eating habits, choosing foods, low health foods, common foods choice eating at cheap restaurant habitual consumption. Also, they have similar entertainment habits, their entertainment demand is not high. They like to ride bicycles to go to anywhere to travel. They like to go to swim, play basketball, football etc. sports. These all sports are cheap sport consumption. So, it based on similar individual low enjoyment demand and low health, food quality demand similar cultural factors. Chinese and Indian people have no long distance cultural difference between eating and entertainment habitual factor will include them to choose to repeat travelling between these both countries. Due to China and India have many restaurants can provide cheap food or sport service providers can provide different kinds of cheap sport entertainment consumption to satisfy their cheap food and cheap entertainment needs in their journey in China or India anywhere. So, it explains that why these both countries tourists will repeat to travel these both countries again after they had visited China or India to travel in first time. So, the similar cultural factor can impact these both countries tourists to repeat to go to these both countries to travel again. Hence, if these two countries' cultural distance is far or different, then themselves countries' tourists won't choose to repeat travel between themselves when these two countries for cultural distance tourists had visited to another country in first time. Hence, culture has been continuously considered as a much factor which tourists consider in terms of choice of the destination travelling place. Also, it explains cultural distance which can make tourist individual has less satisfaction to concern to tourists to repeat travels.

Otherwise, for far cultural distance two countries case example, such as Chinese and American , these two countries people's eating habit and entertainment cultural needs are different. For eating habit difference example, American like to eat pork, beefs, chickens, potato to replace rice and other foods. Otherwise, Chinese like to wat rice, vegetables more than potatoes, pork , beefs for lunch , dinner . So , their eating habits are very different. Also, American like to drive boats on the season drive cars to go to anywhere to travel on holidays for sports or holiday entertainment activities . Otherwise, Chinese like to play basketball, football, ride bicycle of cheaper sport entertainment on holidays. So, American entertainment activities are more expensive to compare Chinese. Also, US and China , like families whose power distance is different, such as every per family powerful member is parents, who have more power to give opinions to choose anywhere to travel for whose sons and/or daughters whole family members travelling arrangement.

Therefore, if the Us family powerful members, such as at least one son or/and daughter members who need t choose to go to which country to travel if the family powerful members, such as the child/ children's parent feel China's food taste or entertainment activities are totally different to be similar to their country's food taste and entertainment activities habitually after their whole family members had travelled to China in first time before. Although, their son(s) and daughter(s) will hope to go to China to repeat travel again. But, due to the US family parents are their son(s) and daughter(S) powerful decider to make any travelling decision to choose which country will be next time travelling destination. If their parents feel China's eating and entertainment culture is totally different to their countries. Then, the US family will not choose to repeat travel to the China country again any more easily, because this US family can not feel satisfactory when they visited China in their first time before, due to they feel China 's food and entertainment cultures are totally different to their US country. So, the cultural distance factor will influence the US family don't choose China to go repeat travel again.

Consequently, different countries' similar or different cultural factor will influence the country's tourists choose to repeat travel to the country again. So, any country needs to know what its culture is in order to attract the similar cultural countries tourists to repeat travel to itself country more easily.

    ● Long time lifestyle factor influences travel
behavior

Whether do different countries tourists' different lifestyle which can influence their travel consumption behaviors? Even, which countries that they will choose to go to travel. For example, when one tourist who owns himself/herself often to drive to go to anywhere habitually. The tourist's driving car habital behavior which will influence that he /she will feel need to rent car to travel to anywhere habitually , when he/she selects to go to the country to travel. Hence, if he/she feels the tourism destination has no any rent car service providers to provide him/her to rent any car to travel anywhere in the country's travel destination. Does the country lack rent car service factor which will influence that he/she will still choose to go to the country to travel in preference? For example, when one New Zealander's family who own at least one car at home. So, the New Zealand whole family every member can often drive car to go to anywhere , even, one family member had driven one car to leave his/her home. So, driving own car activity or behavior has been one habitual activity to influence the New Zealand every member to feel the travelling destination needs have rent car service provider supplies cars to let them to rent to travel. The driving car lifestyle has caused the whole New Zealander family driving habit. When the family's sons) and/or daughter(s) need(s) to go to school or go to shopping as well as their parents also need to drive their cars to go to office to work in themselves home town often. In common, there are many New Zealanders who will have at least one car at home because they feel that they can drive their themselves cars to go to anywhere in New Zealand more than waiting bus or tram or train or ferry etc. public transportation tools more conveniently. So, New Zealanders' driving own car habit will influence their lifestyle to feel that they also need to rent cars to travel to go to any where to travel to replace to wait public transportation tools choice in the travelling destination during their journey.

For shopping trips is more influenced by their driving car activities. So, it seems that this New Zealander families will be influenced to their tourism destination need, they need the tourism destination has car renting service provider to be supplied anywhere to let them can drive the renting cars to go to anywhere in tourism destination. It means that when the tourism destination has less rent car providers can provide renting car services to drive anywhere or it has none any renting car service providers are existing in the tourism destination. Then, the renting car service providers number shortage or none any renting car service providers to be provided to the country's tourism destination, which will cause the New Zealander families do not prefer to choose to go to the country to travel generally, e.g. Hong Kong, China, Korea these Asia countries have no many rent car service providers in these countries. So, the New Zealand families won't prefer to choose to go these countries to travel when they discover these Asia countries lack enough rent car service providers to let them to drive to travel in themselves conveniently. Otherwise, America, England, Japan etc. countries have many rent car service providers. So, these countries will be this New Zealander families' preferable tourism countries. Thus, the New Zealand families' driving ownership car lifestyle will influence their travel behaviors to choose to go to the country which can have many rent car providers in the tourism country any where tourism destinations in preference.

Thus, whether the country has renting car service providers , it will be variable factor to influence any country's car ownership families' driving car travel behaviors in their journey in order to let they feel that they can drive themselves ownership cars to go to anywhere to travel conveniently, even when they leave their countries. Hence, these countries' car ownership driving habitual families' behaviors will be influenced their tourism destination or location decision choice when the country has many renting car service providers in preference as well as this renting car service provider supplying factor will be more important to influence the habitual driving own car traveller to be preferable choice to compare other factors, e.g. cheap entertainment consumption providers factor which include cheap hotel living fee, cheap food price consumption etc. expenditure in the travelling country.

Thus, it explains that different countries' car ownership tourists , whose driving own car activities will cause their daily lifestyles, then their daily driving own car lifestyles will influence their tourism destination choices indirectly. So, it seems that lifestyle can be a outcome variable (or dependent variable) factor to influence travel behavior in any travelling built environment. The travelling built environment characteristics can include density measures (population density, job density), job-housing density). These travelling built environment factor can represent what the city resident's lifestyle. For example, where the location in relation to local center or regional center to the country's residents are living. This country resident's living location will cause this country resident's lifestyles , e.g. holiday or leisure whether it is low budget, active and adventurous or frequent traveller with second place or self-organized , family oriented or close to home. Hence, the country's living built environment will influence the country's resident's lifestyles. Due to different countries' residents will have different lifestyles. Hence, built environments and life styles have relationship to influence every country's residents when they need to go to other countries to travel in their holidays. For example, frequent travellers are usually living in big and busy cities, otherwise, non -frequent travellers are usually living in the country sides, where there are less offices or factories are built to let people to work. So, big city will bring busy feeling to the country's residents, then they will be influenced to feel need to often to go to travel for leisure intention in their holidays. Otherwise, countryside will bring not busy or quiet environment feeling to the country's residents, then they won't feel working feeling when they are living in county side. So, they won't feel need to go t o anywhere to travel in their holidays often.

Hence, built environment will bring either busy or not busy (quiet environment feeing) to the both different country residents when they are living in the places. Their living places will cause their lifestyles are different. Then, they will be influences to feel have more frequent travelling needs or less frequent travelling needs to explain why every country people will have more or less frequent travelling needs.

● Long time peer-to-peer staying
accommodation need impacts
business tourism pattern

I shall explain how any why peer-to-peer accommdation can attract business tourisms to choose business tourism intention? Usually , employees or employers buy business trips, why they choose one particular travelling company over another and why the business tourists choose to travel when the peer (more than one business tourists) who will choose to peer-to-per accommodation business tourism pattern more than the more expensive hotel living comfortable feeling business tourism pattern.

Business travel agents need to know or understand what reasons the employer or employee feels peer-to-peer accommodation business tourism motivation is more suitable or better to compare hotel living comfortable feeling business tourism pattern. Why can business tourism accommodation choice factor influence the business tourist's business trip choice.

Business trip means work related travel to an irregular place or work and it represents that one employee or more than on employees business tourists whose expenses are paid by the business ,he or she or they work(s) for. So, in employer's business trip expense view point, he/she expects the employee or employees can choose the most cheap expenses for whose business trip. It also means that the employer does not expect that it is a high quality journey for the employee's or employees' business trip. The business tourism is year-round, peaking in spring and autumn , but still with high levels of activity in the summer and winter months. It may be long time or short time, e.g. less than one month or more than one month, even more than half year for the business trip. When the employee is employees are working permanent full time employment. It is not for leisure intention, it means that the employer does not hope employee or employees spend(s) extra more expense to spend any leisure or goes (go) to any destinations to visit in their/her/his whole business trip.

Hence, it is based on the cheap expenses for the business trip aim, employer usually demands employees or employees to choose the peer-to-peer be cheaper accommodation to live or the employer will help its employee(s) to choose the peer-to-peer cheaper accommodation to live. So, it seems that expensive hotel living facilities won't be the preferable accommodation choice for employer because the business trip pay or reimburse the employee. Hence, business travel agencies ought not help the business tourists to choose expensive travel package, e.g. expensive hotel accommodation on the trip, expensive transportation tools, e.g. taxi renting service to get to business meetings, the cheap peer-to-peer cheap hostel accommodation and cheap transportation tool, e.g. travel buses pre-booking service, or cheap restaurant choice vacation incentives package is more attractive to let them/him/her to choose for their/her/his business trip.

A business person or a peer-to-peer business people also have /her expect to take advantage of frequent flyer schemes which allow him/her/them to take leisure trip with airlines when they/he/she is /are accumulated sufficient miles in the cheap or air ticket(s) to catch air plane for business trip. Hence, he/she /they expect(s) to earn airlines expenses from whose frequent flyer schemes when they/he/she can claim to original air ticket price from whose employer, but in fact, peer-to-peer business tourists or individual business tourist pay lesser air ticket charge from whose frequent flying program accumulated sufficient miles, even no any payment. So, airlines can benefit the business traveller, such as improved in competition millages programs, quick check in and online check in, lounges with broadband connection etc. service.

Why does peer-to-peer accommodation living factor is the most influential to any business tourist(s) to choose the travel agent? In employer's business trip expensive view point, if it has many employees need to go to other countries business trips for long days frequently. Then, the employer will consider whether the every day accommodation living cost is expensive or not. So, comparison hotel and peer-to-peer hotel price, hotel accommodation price is usually higher than small accommodation rent price. When peer-to-peer accommodation has been shown to positively impact to business trip employers in popular. Because any business spending will be one important considerable factor to influence employers to choose. However, the accommodation renting price will be more influential to impact business tourism cost. Hence, employers will estimate every whole business trip expenses how it can impact peer-to-peer or hotel accommodation choice. So, the living budget factor will be one important influential factor to influence any employers how to choose where are the suitable destination for every individual business tourist or peer-to-peer group business tourists to live. So, it seems small size peer-to-peer accommodation are compared to large size expensive hotels more suitable for business tourists.

Although, it is possible that individual employee or a group peer-to-peer employees will feel peer-to-peer accommodation is not more safe than hotel accommodation. But, their/his/her employer usually does not consider safety, comfortable environment issue for their/his/her every business trip. They only consider lose accommodation price issue. So, the accommodation choice will be one critical factor to influence employers how to help their individual employee or a group peer-to-peer employees to choose where he/she/they will live when he/she/they arrive(s) the destination for whose every business trip. Hence, it seems that accommodation will be one critical factor to influence anywhere to be chosen to live for any business trips to their individual employee or group peer-to-peer employees' needs.

● Long time social , cultural , personal psychological factors influence local tourists'destination choice

What are the main internal and external factors to influence local tourist's domestic travelling choice behaviors and destination choice decision making? What are the social , cultural , personal psychological factors to influence the decision-making of local tourists to travel to different types of tourism destinations in domestic travelling destinations, e.g. attractions, available amenities, image price external factors. They can influence local tourist's destination choice behaviors. Does the individual occupational reason can influence local tourist's local destination travelling choice? So, any travel agents need to develop and promote of domestic destination need to determine the factors influencing tourist's destination choice.

In a local destination tourist individual productive way, how local tourism agents can bring what factors to influence or charge whose local destination travelling behavioral changes. For example, tourist individual behavior and destination choice factor, the comparison between the current local tourism destinations choice and the past local tourism destinations choice factor. Instead of local different travelling destination prices comparison, journeys comparison . What are the other internal and external factor to influence the local tourist's travelling destinations choices behaviors, e.g. attending local festivals, events, taste local cuisine and be part of unique features of a destination. These will be valuable external or internal factors to influence the local tourist's local destinations choices. So, different countries' local travelling destinations will need have a number of key elements that attract visitors and meet their needs. The key elements may include , for example, primary activities, physical setting and social / cultural attributes primary external activities elements, and secondary elements may include catering and shopping, and addition elements/accessibility and tourists information providing to local tourists.

Due to local destination tourism must be cheaper than overseas or foreign destination tourism. So, the local tourist travel agents need to provide their travelling services to local tourists, more attractions, accessibility , amenities, excellent available packages activities and ancillary services to compare overseas tourism destinations. Because the local tourists will compare the overseas different destinations travelling places to decide whether they ought choose to travel overseas or local different destinations at the moment. So, any entertainment activities concern local destinations which will be local tourists' preferable comparative travelling services to the local travel agent and the overseas travelling service in order to decide whether he/she ought choose local travelling or overseas travelling at the moment.

Hence, local different travelling destinations attractive factor will be one important influential factor to influence local tourist's travelling choices. However, a tourist's attitude, decisions, activities, ideas or travelling experiences evaluating and searching of any tourism service behaviors will influence the final travelling destination choice decision whether he/she ought choose to go to overseas or local travel. He/she will consider how to spend time and money and effort to carry on any kinds of entertainment activities in whose local or overseas journeys. So, the different destination local and overseas internal travelling price and spending entertainment time in journey and spending effort to arranging every travelling entertainment which every will be one considerable issue to compare budget to overseas and local different travelling destinations. If the tourist feel whose country

, e.g. American's local travelling destination budget is spend less than overseas travelling destination too much. Then, the American will choose to local travelling destinations more than overseas travelling destinations and the moment. So, travelling budget will one factor to influence the tourist to choose whether overseas or local travelling.

So, it seems that time, money and effort will be another factor to influence the tourist will be another factor to influence the tourist chooses to go to overseas or local travelling destinations, instead of different travelling entertainment provider choices factor in the local or overseas travelling destinations . Moreover, the tourist's individual income, the local and overseas living condition, formation of cultural and aesthetic tastes, price of local and overseas travelling service and discounts, local and overseas travelling destinations' temperature or weather viable, e.g. number of sunny days, geographical condition, cultural and natural resource, medical tourism etc. external factors will influence the tourist individual final travelling decision to choose either local tourism or overseas tourism entertainment decision.

● Long time tourist individual driving behavior
impacts travel behavior

Does every tourist individual driving behavior influence whose travel behavioral choice? However, individual mobility decisions are possible difficulties for measures aiming at tourist individual travelling behavioral changes and links them to the transport need aspect when the tourist arrives the destination to travel. For example, whether the travelling destination has bus public transportation tool supplies or ferry transportation tool supplies or taxi transportation tool supplied or train or tram etc. different public transportation tools to influence the tourist individual travelling destination choice.

When every country decides to develop travel industry. It needs to understand how to arrange what kind of public transportation tools to be supplied to satisfy any countries' tourists mobility needs in whose journeys in order to achieve tourism planning for public transportation system to attract different countries' tourists to choose to arrive itself different destinations to travel more easily. So, the country's transportation services supplies will have permanently impacted to every tourist individual travel behavior towards more mobility when he/she arrives to the country to travel.

Can transportation system factor influence tourist individual travelling destination decision? it depends on the tourist individual attitude or transport needs of decisions. For example, if the city , e.g. New York has many tourists, who are high income, young gender, high education level tourists. Then, they will choose more expensive and comfortable train more than cheap and not comfortable bus transportation tool. So, I assume that the year has many high income, high education , high social class occupation tourists arrive US , New York city . Then, they will choose train more than bus transportation tool to go to anywhere to travel in New York city. So, it is not represent that the city has many cheaper public transportation tool, such as many buses number to be supplied , the bus public transportation tool can bring more income to attract overseas tourists to come to New York travel. It depends on whether the tourist individual characteristics, e.g. high or low income, more or less comfortable transporation tool supplies needs or high or low educational level, alone tourist or family tourist or friend relationship tourist. Any one of these tourist individual psychological factors will influence the tourist to choose either cheap and less comfortable public tool system or expensive and more comfortable public tool system to be supplied to the city to travel. So, the city's comfortable or not comfortable public transportation tool supplies which will influence the overseas tourists how to choose the city to travel.

However, on the tourist's habitual behavior of catching which kind of transportation tools, this factor will bring to influence how to choose the kind of transportation tool(s) whether the city can provide choice to let the overseas tourist to make where travelling decision when he/she arrives to the country. However, his/her transportation tool catching habit will be possible to influence whose travel times for public transport use, instead of which kind of transport tool(s) he/she will choose to catch when he/she arrives the country to travel.

In conclusion, the tourist's age, income, occupation, education level will influence how the tourist's transportation choice in himself/herself country, then it also bring this question: will influence the tourist individual destination choice if the country can provide or can not provide the kind of public transportation tool(s) to let the tourist to choose to catch in his/her journey in the country's city. Hence, it explains that why every country's pubic transporation tool supplies will influence the tourist to choose where to travel in the country.

● Long time disabled habits
and attitudes influence to disabled tourists' behaviors

What factors can affect the travel behaviors of people with disabilities by ages and lifestyle variable factors? When one person is disable, he/she will have different behaviors to satisfy whose needs in whose whole travelling journey. In special , the older age and younger age disable tourists who will have different travelling needs. In fact, the disabled tourists won't easy to go anywhere travelling destinations in whose whole travelling journey. So, it seems that the travelling entertainment needs won't be very much to these younger or older disabled tourists. Moreover, people with disabilities travel will be compare with people without disabilities. So, it is one key to explain why the travelling entertainment purposes or needs to disable people which are lesser than the people without disabilities.

In negative or problematic experience of travel to disabled tourists aspect, I believe that it is one travelling experiences problem is considered to need to be solved to any younger or older age disabled tourists, because they are handicapped people, they will feel walk in difficulty, even they need wheel chairs to help them to walk. So, the moving disabled problem will influence how they feel unsafe on public transport in any strange travelling countries considerable. In special, the older aged 50 and over disabled people need to catch any public transport when they need to sit on wheel chairs to go to anywhere destinations in any strange travelling countries. They will feel not convenient and unsafe when they need to sit on wheel chairs to go to anywhere destinations. These travelling places are their first time arriving places. Hence, transportation tools will be consideration problem to any disabled tourists. It seems that renting car travelling providers will be one popular or preferable choice to any younger orolder age disabled tourists. Because disabled tourists won't need to catch public transport tools, such as buses, trains, trams, taxis in unsafe, notconvenient natural travelling environment. They can drive themselves renting cars to go to anywhere travelling destinations easily or conveniently. Thus, I believe that the renting cr travelling service which is very attractive to any young or old age disabled tourist nowadays.

In general, instead of renting cars to drive behavioral change to disabled tourists usually ,renting cars behaviors which will replace to choose to catch any public transportation tools behavior to disable tourists. What kinds of other behavioral changes will impact to disabled tourists? Other aspect consideration is disabled tourist individual health problem . For example, if the disabled tourist is driving himself/herself renting cars to go to anywhere destinations in long term in the travelling country. The long distance of driving miles travelling and driving long hours spend travelling behaviors will influence the disable tourist individual nervous health to be more poor, because he/she needs to spend more time and nervous to drive whose renting car to go to anywhere in whole travelling journey. So, it is very dangerous and unsafe to the disabled tourist when he/she needs to concentrate on nervous to drive himself/herself renting car to go to anywhere destinations to travel in whose travelling journey or trip.

In consideration of the older age disabled tourist groups will be more unsafe and dangerous when he/she needs to spend much time to drive whose renting car to arrive any travelling destinations. So, it is based on this long time unsafe driving factor, the older age disabled tourist groups will choose to spend lesser time to drive to go to anywhere destinations to travel alone or with their friends and/or families in general. Similar patterns are evident in the numbers of miles travelled and the time spent to driving renting car behavior to any older age disabled tourist groups will be lesser than the younger age disabled tourist groups . Due to the long time unsave renting car self-driving feeling to the older age disabled tourists. It will impact to influence the older age disabled tourists to choose to catch any public transport or walking to replace renting car self-driving behaviors in their trips, when older age handicapped tourists loss hearing, sight, memory, recognizing physical danger, personal care difficulties disabled characteristics.

Thus, the long time renting car driving behavior which will influence the old age disabled tourists to choose to catch public transport tools to replace to rent car to drive in whose trip persuasively. So, the renting car providers will have lesser old age disable tourist number to compare to young age disabled tourist number in common. Also, the old age disable tourists will prefer to choose the travel destinations where have many public transport tools to let them to catch for their travelling journeys.

● Long time social internet networking behavior
impacts traveller individual behavior

Can web site online internet networking influence traveller individual behavior changes? If web site can influence every online traveller user individual behavior change, how it influence every online user individual behavior change in order to impact his/her travelling service or arrangement change choice. For example, when the traveller walks in one travel agent's shop to find the most suitable travelling package for whose trip.

At the moment, he/she plans to find the travel agent to help him/her to arrange any travelling package. But when he/she goes back his/her home, he/she turns on his/her computer to link online travel agent website. Then, he/she discovers this online travel agent can provide more attractive travelling package similar service and he/she will compare the walk in travel agent's travelling package to this online travel agent travelling package. Although, the walk-in travelling agent can provide lesser service fee to compare this online travel agent. But , he/she feels this online travel agent can provide more attractive and enjoyable travelling entertainment and trip arrangement service to satisfy his/her travelling need. So, he/she decides to choose this online travelling agent's travelling package and it seems that the online travel agent web site can influence his/her original travelling agent target choice.

Nowadays, the most famous online development reshaping traditional marketing methods of tourism business will be possible to replace the traditional walk-in travel agent business. Because travelling consumers like to turn on computer to link to different travelling agents' websites to choose which travelling package is the cheapest or it can provide the most attractive or enjoyable entertainment arrangement in the trip. So, online travel agents will influence travelling consumers to reduce to spend time to walk in to visit any travel agent shops. The traveller prefers to spend much time to find which travelling agents' websites to find the most right online travelling agent to help him/her to arrange the trip service to replace to find the most right walk-in travelling agent at home conveniently. So, travelling agent website development can impact every traveller individual planning behavior to be changed influentially because when he/she plans to walk in to visit the identified travel agent shop, but when he/she has one desk top computer to be installed at home. Then, he/she will have another choice to buy the travelling package service. So, he/she will change his/her walk in to visit the travel agent planning behavior to change to clicking on any travel agent's website behavior.

Moreover, travelling website characteristics or attractive point is easy communication. When the traveller feels any worry or trouble, he/her need to enquire the online travelling agent immediately. He/she can send email to enquire the travelling agent to arrange travelling package similar service to walk in travel agent and he/she will compare the walk in travel agent's travelling package to this online travel agent travelling package.

Although, the walk-in travelling agent can provide lesser service fee to compare this online travel agent. But, he/she feels that this online travel agent can provide more attractive and enjoyable travelling entertainment and trips service to satisfy his/her travelling need. So, he/she decides to choose this online travelling agent's travelling package and it seems that the online travel agent website can influence his/her original travelling agent target choice.

Nowadays, the most famous online development reshaping traditional marketing methods of tourism business will be possible to replace the traditional walk-in travel agent business. Because travelling walk-in consumer like to turn on computer to link to different travelling agents' websites to choose which travelling package is the cheapest or it can provide the most attractive or enjoyable entertainment arrangement .

Thus, online travelling information search tool can attract travellers to choose to find any travel agents' websites from internet to replace walk-in travel agents' shops influentially. Also, it seems online travelling service will be popular to replace walk-in travelling service in possible.

● Long time cultural distance on satisfaction and
respect travel intention

Every country cultural difference is different. How and why cultural difference has a real impact on tourist satisfaction and it can also influence to repeat travel. Is cultural tourism one major factor to influence tourist to repeat travelling intention or choice to the country in international tourism choice market? For example, China and India have similar culture. Their cultural difference is not much, e.g. eating cultural habit is similar , entertainment cultural habit is similar. These both countries people do not want to spend much money in eating and entertainment both aspects. Hence, these two countries people do not consider how to consume to enjoy entertainment and eat expensive food. Hence, it is based on cultural similar reason. These both countries tourists will prefer to choose to repeat travelling either China or India. When the Indian tourists had chosen to go to China to travel in the first time. Then, the Indian tourists will choose to go to China to travel in second time again. Also, the Indian tourists had chosen to go to China to travel in first time. Then, the Chinese tourists will choose to go to India to travel in second time again.

What factors influence China and India touists repect to travel between these both countries. The factors will include cheap air ticket price, cheap hotel living price , less economic cost factor. However, I believe the similar cultural factor will be the major factor to influence many Chinese and Indian tourist prefer to choose to repeat travelling between these both countries.

As my indication to these both countries people have similar eating habits, choosing foods, low health foods, common foods choice eating at cheap restaurant habitual consumption. Also, they have similar entertainment habits, their entertainment demad is not high. They like to ride bicycles to go to anywhere to travel. They like to go to swim, play backetball, football etc. sports. These all sports are cheap sport consumption. So, it based on similar individual low enjoyment dcmand and low health, food quality demand similar cultural factors. Chinese and Indian people have no long distance cultural difference between eating and entertainment habitual factor will include them to choose to repeact travelling between these both countries. Due to China and India have many restaurants can provide cheap food or sport service providers can provide diffent kinds of cheap sport entertainment consumption to satisfy their cheap food and cheap entertainment needs in their journey in China or India anywhere. So, it explains that why these both countries tourists will repeat to travel these both countries again after they had visited China or India to travel in first time. So, the similar cultural factor can impact these both countries tourists to repeat to go to these both countries to travel again. Hence, if these two countries' cultural distance is far or different, then themselves countries' tourists won't choose to repeat travel between themselves when these two countries for cultural distance toutists had visited to another country in first time. Hence, culture has been continuously considered as a much factor which tourists consider in terms of choice of the destination travelling place. Also, it explains cultural distance which can make tourist individual has less satisfaction to concern to tourists to repeat travels.

Otherwise, for far cultural distance two countries case example, such as Chinese and American , these two countries people's eating habit and entertainment cultural needs are different. For eating habit difference example, American like to eat poks, beefs, chickens, potatos to replace rice and other foods. Otherwise, Chinese like to wat rice, vegatables more than potatoes, porks , beefs for lunch , dinner . So , their eating habits are very different. Also, American like to drive boats on the seasor drive crs to go to anywhere to travel on holidays for sports or holiday entertainment activities . Otherwise, Chinese like to play backetball, football, ride bicycle of cheaper sport entertainment on holidays. So, American entertainment activities are more expensive to compare Chinese. Also, US and China , like families whose power distance is dfferent, such as every per family powerful member is parents, who have more power to give opinions to choose anywhere to travel for whose sons and/or daughters whole familily members travelling arrangement.

Therefore, if the Us family powerful members, such as at least one son or/ and ond daughter members who need t choose to go to which country to travel if the family powerful members, such as the child/ children's parent feel China's food taste or entertainment activities are totally different to be similar to their country's food taste and entertainment activities habitually after their whole fmily members had travelled to China in first time before. Although, their son(s) and daughter(s) will hope to go to China to repect travel again. But, due to the US family parents are their son(s) and daughter(S) powerful decider to make any travelling decision to choose which country will be next time travelling destination. If their parents feel China's eating and entertainment culture is totally different to their countries. Then, the US family will not choose to repeat travel to the China country again any more easily, beause this US family can not feel satisfactory when they visited China in their first time before, due to they feel China 's food and entertainment cultures are totally different to their US country. So, the cultural distance factor will influence the US family don't choose China to fo repeat travel again.

Consequently, different countries' similar or different cultural factor will influence the country's tourists choose to repeact travel to the country again. So, any country needs to know what its culture is in order to attract the similar cultural countries tourists to repeat travel to itself country more easily.

● Long time lifestyle habit influences travel
behavior

Whether do different countries tourists' different lifestyle which can influence their travel consumption behaviors? Even, which countries that they will choose to go to travel. For example, when one tourist who owns himself/herself often to drive to go to anywhere habitually. The tourist's driving car habital behavior which will influence that he /she will feel need to rent car to travel to anywhere habitually , when he/she selects to go to the country to travel. Hence, if he/she feels the tourism destination has no any rent car service providers to provide him/her to rent any car to travel anywhere in the country's travel destination. Does the country lack rent car service factor which will influence that he/she will still choose to go to the country to travel in preference? For example, when one New Zealander's family who own at least one car at home. So, the New Zealand whole family every member can often drive car to go to anywhere , even, one family member had driven one car to leave his/her home. So, driving own car activity or behavior has been one habitual activity to influence the New Zealand every member to feel the travelling destination needs have rent car service provider supplies cars to let them to rent to travel. The driving car lifestyle has caused the whole New Zealander family driving habit. When the family's sons) and/or daughter(s) need(s) to go to school or go to shopping as well as their parents also need to drive their cars to go to office to work in themselves home town often. In common, there are many New Zealanders who will have at least one car at home because they feel that they can drive their themselves cars to go to anywhere in New Zealand more than waiting bus or tram or train or ferry etc. public transportation tools more conveniently. So, New Zealanders' driving own car habit will influence their lifestyle to feel that they also need to rent cars to travel to go to any where to travel to replace to wait public transportation tools choice in the travelling destination during their journey.

For shopping trips is more influenced by their driving car activities. So, it seems that this New Zealander families will be influenced to their tourism destination need, they need the tourism destination has car renting service provider to be supplied anywhere to let them can drive the renting cars to go to anywhere in tourism destination. It means that when the tourim destination has less rent car providers can provide renting car services to drive anywhere or it has none any renting car service providers are existing in the tourism destination. Then, the renting car service providers number shortage or none any renting car service providers to be provided to the country's tourism destination, which will cause the New Zealander families do not perfer to choose to go to the country to travel generally, e.g. Hong Kong, China, Korea these Asia countries have no many rent car service providers in these countries. So, the New Zealand families won't prefer to choose to go these countries to travel when they discover these Asia countries lack enough rent car service providers to let them to drive to travel in themselves conveniently. Otherwise, America, England, Japan etc. countries have many rent car service providers. So, these countries will be this New Zealander families' preferable tourism countries. Thus, the New Zealand families' driving ownership car lifestyle will influence their travel behaviors to choose to go to the country which can have many rent car providers in the tourism country any where tourism destinations in preference.

Thus, whether the country has renting car service providers , it will be variable factor to influence any country's car ownship families' driving car travel behaviors in their journey in order to let they feel that they can drive themselves ownship cars to go to anywhere to travel conveniently, even when they leave their countries. Hence, these countries' car ownship driving habitual families' behaviors will be influenced their tourism destination or location decision choice when the country has many renting car service providers in preference as well as this renting car service provider supplying factor will be more important to influence the habitual driving own car traveller to be preferable choice to compare other factors, e.g. cheap entertainment consumption providers factor which include cheap hotel living fee, cheap food price consumption etc. expenditure in the travelling country.

Thur, it explains that different countries' car ownship tourists , whose driving own car activities will cause their daily lifestyles, then their daily driving own car lifestyles will influence their tourism destination choices indirectly. So, it seems that lifestyle can be a outcome variable (or dependent variable) factor to influence travel behavior in any travelling built environment. The travelling built environment characteristics can include density measures (population density, job density), job-housing density). These travelling buit environment factor can repreent what the city resident's lifestyle. For example, where the location in relation to local centre or regional centre to the country's residents are living. This country resident's living location will cause this country resident's lifestyles , e.g. holiday or leisure whether it is low budget, active and adventurous or frequent traveller with second place or self-orgnized , family oriented or close to home and unadventurour. Hence, the country's living built environment will influence the country's resident's lifestyles. Due to different countries' residents will have different lifestyles. Hence, built environments and lifestlyes have relationship to influence every country's residents when they need to go to other countries to travel in their holidays. For example, frequent travellers are usually living in big and busy cities, otherwise, non -frequent travellers are ususaly living in the countrysides, where there are less offices or factories are built to let people to work. So, big city will bring busy feeling to the country's residents, then they will be influenced to feel need to often to go to travel for leisure intention in their holidays. Otherwise, countryside will bring not busy or quiet environment feeling to the country's residents, then they won't feel working feeling when they are living in counryside. So, they won't feel need to go t o anywhere to travel in their holidays often.

Hence, built environment will bring either busy or not busy (quiet environment feeing) to the both different country residents when they are living in the places. Their living places will cause their lifestyles are different. Then, they will be influences to feel have more frequent travelling needs or less frequent travelling needs to explain why every country people will have more or less frequent travelling needs.

● Time factor influences travel behavioural consumption

How to predict travel consumption by time factor? It is one question to any travel agents concern how to use past time and future time to predict how many numbers of travelers where who will choose to go to travel more accurately. I think that who can consider how to predict travel behavioral consumption from psychology view and computer science view both.

On the psychology view, It has evidence to support the relationship between self-identify threat and resistance to change travel behavior to any travelers, controlling for whose past travelling behavior, resistance to change if a psychological phenomenon of long standing interest in many applied branches of psychology. Past travelling behavior has been acknowledged as a predictor of future action. Such as travelling behavior that is experienced as successful is likely to be repeated and may lead to habitual patterns. Some psychologists differentiate habit between two concepts, such as goal oriented and automatic oriented both. Although repeated past travelling behavior is addition goal oriented and automatic oriented. Further non-deliberative nature of habit may make appeals to judge and to predict future individual traveler's behaviour accrately. However, repeated travelling behavior without a necessary constraint of goal orientation and automatic oriented both. So, it seems that the traveller's past travelling experience time psychological factor can influence any individual traveler why and how who choose to decide whose travelling behaviour.

● Can the country's past travel time climate change factor influence travelling behaviours?

The flexibility of human travelling behavior is at least the result of one such mechanism, our ability to travel mentally in time and entertain potential future. Understanding of the impacts is holidays, particularly those involving travel. Using focus groups research to explores tourists' awareness of the impacts of travel own climate change, examines the extent to which climate change features in holiday travel decisions and identifies some of the barriers to the adoption of less carbon intensive tourism practices. The findings suggest many tourists don't consider climate change when planning their holidays. The failure of tourists to engage with the climate change to impact of holidays, combined with significant barriers to behavioral change, presents a considerable challenge in the tourism industry.

Tourism is a highly energy intensive industry and has only recently attracted attention as an important contributions to climate change through greenhouse gas emissions. It has been estimated that tourism contributes 5% of global carbon dioxide emissions. There have been a number of potential changes proposed for reducing the impact of air travel on climate change. These include technological changes, market based changes and behavioral changes. However, the role that climate change plays in the holiday and travel decisions of global tourists. How the global tourists of the impacts travel has on climate change to establish the extent to which climate change, considerations features in holiday travel decision making processes and to investigate the major barriers to global tourists adopting less carbon intensive travel practices. Whether tourists will aware the impacts that their holidays and travel have on climate changes.

When, it comes to understand indvidual traveler's behavioral change, wide range of conceptual theories have been developed, utilizing various social, psychological, subjective and objective variables in order to model travel consumption behavior. These theories of travel behavioral change operate at a number of different levels, including the individual level, the interpersonal level and community level. Whether pro-environmental behavior can be used to predict travel consumption behavior in a climate change. However, the question of what determines pro-environmental behavior in such a complex one that it can not be visualized through one single framework or diagram.

Despite the potentially high risk scenario for the tourism industry and the global environment, the tourism and climate change ought have close relationship. Whether what are the important factors and variables which can limit tourism? e.g. money, time, family problem, extreme hot or cold weather change, air ticket price, journey attraction etc. variable factors. Mention of holidays and travel were deliberately avoided in the recruitment process, so as not to create a connection factor to influence traveler's individual mind. However, the dismissal of alternative transportation modes can be conceived as either a structural barrier, in the sense that flying is perhaps the only realistic option to reach long-haul holiday destination, or a perceived behavioral control barriers in that an individual perceives flying as the only option open to whom. The transportation tool factor will be depend to extent on the distance to the destination. This can also be interpreted in a social perspective as an intention with the resources available where much international tourism is structured around flying. To increase the availability of different transportation modes, tourists could choose holiday destination closer to home.

Finally, also how to predict future travel behavioural consumption. I feel that travel agents need to predict whether any country's random daily variation of weather factor is also important to influence travel behaviour. e.g. in weather, temperature, rainfall adn snowfall with traffic accidents factors will have relationship to cause travel demand. Some scientists estimate suggest that when warmed temperatures and reduced snowfall are associated with a moderate decline in non-fatal accidents, they are also associated with a significant increase in fatal accidents. Thus increase in fatalities and temperature. Half of the estimated effect of temperature on fatalities is due to changes in the exposure to pedestrians, bicyclists and motorcyclists as temperature increase. So, if any countries have rainfall, snowfall and low temperature to cause traffic accidents, whether this accident occurrence will influence the travelers who liking climb snow hills, riding bicycle, running sports who will avoid to travel to these countries' bad weather after occurs. So, why I feel that this natural climate factor will also be one serious factor to influence travel behavioral consumption.

● Can the traveller's past travelling time entertainment experience factor predict future travel consumption behavior?

Whether individual habitual behaviour can influence travelling behaviour :

e.g. renting travel transportation tools

Whether habit can be intended to predict of future travel behavior to people are creatures of habits. Many of human's everyday goal-directed behaviors are performed in a habitual fashion, the transportation made and route one takes to work, one's choice of breakfast. Habits are formed when using the some behavior frequently and a similar consistency in a similar context for the some purpose whether the individual past travel consumption model will be caused a habit to whom. e.g. choosing whom travel agent to buy air ticket or traveling package; choosing the same or similar countries' destinations to go to travel ; choosing the business class or normal (general) class of quality airlines to catch planes. Does habitual rent traveling car tools use not lead to more resistance to change of travel mode? It has been argued that past behavior is the best predictor of future behavior to travel consumption. If individual traveler's past consumption behavior was always reasoned, then frequency of prior travel consumption behavior should only have an indirect link to the individual traveler's behavior. It seems that renting travel car tools to use is a habit example. So, a strong rent traveling car tools useful habit makes traveling mode choice. People with a strong renting of traveling car tools of habit should have low motivation to attend to gather any information about public transportation in their choice of travelling country for individual or family or friends members during their traveling journeys.

Even when persuasive communication changes the traveler whose attitudes and intention, in the case of individual traveler or family travelers with a strong renting travel car tools habit. It is difficult to change whose travel behaviors to choose to catch public transportation in whose any trips in any countries. However, understanding of travel behavior and the reasons for choosing one mode of transportation over another. The arguments for rent traveling car tools to use, including convenience, speed, comfort and individual freedom and well known. Increasingly, psychological factors include such as, perceptions, identity, social norms and habit are being used to understand travel mode choice. Whether how many travel consumers will choose to rent traveling car tools during their trips in any countries. It is difficult to estimate the numbers. As the average level of renting travel car tools of dependence or attitudes to certain travel package policies from travel agents. Instead different people must be treated in different ways because who are motivated in different ways and who are motivated by different travel package policies ways from travel agents.In conclusion, the past and present and future travelling entertainment time experience factors can influence whose traveler's individual behavior either who chooses to rent traveling car tools or who chooses to catch public transportation when who individual goes to travel in alone trip or family trip. It include influence mode choice factors, such as social psychology factor and marketing on segmentation factor both to influence whose transportation choice of behavior in whose trip.

● How to determine future travel behavior from past travel time experience and perceptions of risk and safety for the benefits to travel consumers?

How to determine future travel behavior from past travel experience and perceptions of risk and safety for the benefits to travel consumers? Why does individual traveler avoid certain destination(s) is(are) as relevant to tourist decision making as why who chooses to travel to others. Perceptions of risk and safety and travel experience are likely to influence travel decisions. If travel agents had efforts to predict future travel behavior to guess whether travelers will feel where is(are) risk and unsafe to cause who does not choose to go to the country to travel. Then, the travel agents will avoid to choose to spend much time to design the different traveling package to attract their potential travel consumers to choose to travel. The reason is because in the case of individual traveler's tourism experience, the traveler whose past disappointment travel experience (psychological risk) will be a serious threat to the traveler's health or life (health, physical or terrorism risk). The past safety or unhealthy risk to the country(countries) will influence the traveler decides to choose not to go to the countries(country) to travel again in the future.

● What is past travelling experience time push and pull factors influence any traveler who chooses where is whose preferable travelling destination

How to predict individual traveler's behavioral intention of choosing a travel destination. Understanding why people travel and what factors influence their behavioral intention of choosing a travel destination is beneficial to tourism planning and marketing. In general, an individual's choice of a travel destination into two forces. The first force is the push factor that pushes an individual away from home and attempt to develop a general desire to go somewhere, without specifying where that may be. The other force is the pull factor that pull an individual toward in destination, due to a region-specific or perceived attractiveness of a destination. The respective push and pull factors illustrate that people travel because who are pushed by whose internal motives and pulled by external forced of a destination. However, the decision making process leading to the choice of a travel destination is a very complex process. For example, a Taiwanese traveler who might either choose new travel destination of Hong Kong or another old travel Asia destinations again or who also might choose any one of Western country, as a new travel destination. The travel agents can predict where who will have intention to choose to travel from whose past behavior and attitude, subjective and perceived behavioral control model.

The factors influence where is the traveler choice, include personal safety, scenic beauty, cultural interest, climate changing, transportation tools, friendliness of local people, price of trip, trip package service in hotels and restaurants, quality and variety of food and shopping facilities and services etc. needs. So, whose factors will influence where is the individual travel's choice. It seems every traveler whose choice of travel process, will include past behavior. e.g. travelling experience, travelling habit, then to choose the best seasoned travelling action to satisfy whose travel needs. This process is the individual traveler's psychological choice process, who must need time to gather information to compare concerning of different travel packages, destination scene, climate change, transportation tools available to the destination, air ticket price etc. these factors, then to judge where is the best right destination to travel in the right time.

● Why past travelling time expectation, motivation and attitude factor can influence travelling behaviour?

Social psychology is concerned with gaining insight into the psychological of socially relevant behaviors and the processes. For instance, on a global level bad influence to global warming, it influences some countries extreme cold or hot bad climate changing occurrence, then it ought influence some travelers' behavioral decision to change their mind to choose some countries to go to travel at the moment which do not occur extreme hot or cold climate (temperature). e.g. above than 40 degree in summer or below than 0 degree in winter. Due to the extreme climate changing environment in the countries, it will cause them to feel uncomfortable to play during their trips. So, the global warming causes to climate changing factor will influence the numbers of travel consumption to be reduced possibly. This is global climate changing environment factor influences to bad or uncomfortable social psychological feeling to global travelers' mind of traveling decision. What is individual traveler expectation, motivation and attitude? Tourism sector includes inbound (domestic) tourism and outbound (overseas) tourism both incomes to any countries. According to recent article, a tourist behavior model has been developed, called the expectation, motivation and attitude (EMA) model (Hsu et al., 2010).

This model focuses on the pre-visit stage of tourists by modeling the behavioral process by incorporating expectation, motivation and attitude. Travel motivation is considered as an essential component of the behavioral process, which has been increasing attention from the travel; industry. The economic approach defines "tourism" is an identifiable nationally important industry. It includes the component activities of transportation, accommodation, recreation, food and related service. So, tourism behavioral consumption is concerned the individual tourist's usual habituate of the industry which responds to whose needs, and of the impacts that both the tourist and the tourism industry have on the socio-cultural, economic and physical environment.

However, travel motivation means how to understand and predict factors that influence travel decision making. According to Backman and others (1995, p.15), motivation is conceptually viewed as " a state of need, a condition that services as a driving force to display different kind of behavior toward certain types of activities, developing preferences, arriving at some expected satisfactory outcome." So, motivation and expectancy which has close relationship to any tourist before who decided to do any tourism of behavior. Some economists confirmed motivation and expectancy which has relations, such as expectation of visiting an outbound destination has a direct effect on motivation to visit the destination; motivation has a direct effect on attitude toward visiting the destination; expectation of visiting the outbound destination has a direct affect on attitude toward visiting the destination and motivation has a mediating effect on the relationship in between expectation and attitude.

How can apply past travelling entertainment experience time factor to predict future travel behavioural consumption?

I also suggest to use qualitative of travel behavioural method to predict future travel consumption. Methods such as focus groups interviews and participant observer techniques can be used with quantitative approaches on their own to fill the gaps left by quantitative techniques. These insights have contributed to the development of increasingly sophisticated models to forecast travel behavior and predict changes in behavior in response to change in the transportation system. First, survey methods restrict not only the question frame but the answer frame as well, anticipating the important issues and questions and the responses. However, these surveys methods are not well suited to exploratory areas of research where issues remain unidentified and the researched seek to answer the question "why?". Second, data collection methods using traditional travel diaries or telephone recruitment can under represent certain segments of the population, particularly the older persons with little education, minorities and the poor. Before the survey, focus group for example can be used to identify what socio-demographic variables to include in the survey, how best to structure the diary, even what incentives will be most effective in increasing the response rate. After the survey, focus, focus groups can be used to build explanations for the survey results to identify the "why" of the results as well as the implications. One Asia Pacific survey research result was made by tourism market investigation before. It indicated the travel in Asia Pacific market in the past, had often been undertaken in large groups through leisure package sold in bulk, or in large organized business groups, future travelers will be in smaller groups or alone, and for a much wider range of reasons. Significant new traveler segments, such as female business traveler. The small business traveler and the senior traveler, all of which have different aspirations and requirements from the travel experience.

Moreover, Asia tourism market will start to exist behaviors in the adoption of newer technologies, a giving the traveler new ways to manage the travel experience, creating new behaviors. This with provide new opportunities for travel providers. The use of mobile devices, smartphones, tablets etc. and social media are the obvious findings to become an integral part of the travel experience. Thus, quality method can attempt to predict Asia Pacific tourism market development in the future.

However, improving the predictive power of travel behavior models and to increase understanding travel behavior which lies in the use of panel data(repeated measures from the same individuals). Whereas, cross-sectional data only reveal inter-individual differences at one moment in time, panel data can reveal intra-individual changes over time. In effect, panel data are generally better suited to understand and predict (changes in) travel behavior. However, a substantial proportion was also observed to transition between very different activity/travel patterns over time, indicating that from one year to the next, many people renegotiated their activity/travel patterns.

Nowadays, past travelling experience time information can predict how traveler behavior and network performance will change in the future . For example, when steadily growing levels of vehicle ownership and vehicle miles traveled information has been identified as a potential strategy towards man aging travel demand, optimizing transportation networks and better utilizing available capacity. Toward, this goal to predict further tourist behavioral consumption. Many countries, government tourism development institutes has applied advanced traveler information systems (ATIS) which travel behavior models and high-fidelity network performance models made increasingly feasible through the rapid advances in computer power. Crucial components of this problem domain are the modeling of individual tourist drivers' response to travel information and the development accurate guidance of relevance to real would trip makers. So, this advanced traveler information systems (ATIS) can assist the tourist who like to rent travelling car tools to travel in any countries own free traveler information systems service conveniently. Also, this travel information system can be intended to assist travelers to make better travel choices. e.g. this system can improve the decision making of individual traveler rather than improvements of network performance overall. So, we need to understand how tourists make their travel plans. Also, understanding decision process that lead to booking of the trip is equally important, as it allows of a potential behavior.

● Can gather past online tourism sale information predict future traveling consumption of behaviour?

Nowadays, internet is popular, it seems that booking air ticket behavior of using internet is predicted to influence overall tourism air tickets payment method. Tourism industry has grown in the previous several decades. Despite its global impact, questions related to better understanding of tourists and whose habits. Using online travel air ticket booking benefits include booking electronic air tickets can be made from entering any electronic travel agents websites in the short time and electronic travel ticket payers do not need leave home, who can pay visa card to pre booking any electronic travel ticket from online channel conveniently.

How to analyze activity based travel demand ? Nowadays, human are concerning the traffic congestion and air quality deterioration, the supply oriented focus of transportation planning has expanded to include how to manage travel demand within the available transportation supply.

Consequently, there has been an increasing interest in travel demand management strategies, such as congestion pricing that attempts to change aggregate travel demand. The prediction aggregate level, long term travel demand to understanding disaggregate level (i.e. individual levels) behavioral responses to short term demand policies, such as ride sharing incentives, congestion pricing and employer based demand management schemes, alternate work schedules, telecommuting limitation of travel agent traditionally work nature shall influence oriented trip based travel modelling passenger travel demand indirectly.

Finally, online travel purchase will be popular to influence the number of travel behavioural consumption nowadays. Any travel package products can be sold from websites to attract travellers to choose to prebook air ticket for any trips conveniently. In the past ten years, the internet has become the predominant carrier of all types of information and transactions. Regarding travel decisions, internet has also become an important sales channels for the travel industry, because it is associated with comparably lower distribution and sales costs, but also because ir adapts to hign supply and demand dynamics in this industry. Consequently, the travel and tourism industry tries to increase the internet sale specific share of sales volumes. So, internet sale channel has changed travel consumption behavioural pattern and characteristics and travel experience. For example, Switzerland has one of the highest population-to-computer ratio in Europe. It is also one of the most highly internet penetrated countries in terms of use of the WWW on a day-to-day basis, with more than 75 percent of the population older than 14 years using the WWW daily (ICT, 2005).

The reason of booking online tourism may include: convenience, fast transaction, finding traveling package choice easily, more airline seats available. So, online booking tourism will influence the traditional tourism agents visiting of sales and air tickets and travelling package numbers to be decreased. Finally, the online booking tourism market shares will be expanded to more than traditional tourism agents visits sale market in the future one day. So, the travel agents who still use the traditional tourism visiting sale channel which ought raise whose features to compare to differ to online tourism sale channel if these traditional touriam agents want to keep competitive ability in tourism industry for long term.

● Can gather past urban population of travel behaviour to predict future travel behavior?

Actively based patterns of urban population. It is a method of motivational framework means in which societal constraints and inherent individual motivations interact to shape activity participation patterns. It can be used to predict one city or urban the numbers of travel demand in the year. It has two elements: First, capability constraints refer to constraints are imposed by biological needs, such as eating and sleeping and/or resources, such as income, availability of cars etc. to undertake the urban or city's family activities in the year. Second, coupling constraints define where, when and the duration of planning activities that are to be pursued with other individuals. So, this method needs to gather information (data) to get the relationship between activities, travel and spending work time and space time to evaluate whether there are how many families who have real needs to spend time to go to travel in the year.

What is trip based versus activity based approaches? The fundamental difference between the trip-based and activity based approaches is that the former approach directly focuses on trips without explicit recognition of the motivation or reason for the trips and travel. The activity based approach , on the other hand, views travel as a demand derived from the need to pursue travel activities. So, it is better understand the individual or family behavior basis for individual or family travelling decision regarding participation in travelling activities in certain places or cities or countries at given times and hence the resulting travel needs. This behavioral basis includes all the factors that influence the why, how, when and where of performed activities and resulting individuals and household, the cultural/ social norms of the community and the travel surrounding environment.

Another difference between the two approaches is in the way travel is represented. The trip based approach represents travel as a collection of trips. Each trip is considered as independent of other trips, without considering the inter-relationship in the choice attributes , such as time, destination and mode of different trips. As tours are chains of trips beginning and ending at a same location , say home or work. The tour based representation helps maintain the consistency across and capture the interdependency and consistency of the modeled choice attributed among the trips of the same tour.

In addition to the tour based representation of travel, the activity based approach focuses on sequences or patterns of activity participation and travel behavior, using the whole day or longer periods of time is the unit of analysis. Such as approach can address travel demand management issues through an examination of how people modify their activity participation, for example, will individuals substitute more out-of-home activities for in home activities in the evening of who arrived early form work due-to a work schedule change?

The major difference between trip based and the activity based approaches is in the way, the time dimension of activities and travel is considered. In the trip based approach, time is reduced to being simply a cost making a trip and a day's viewed as a combination, defined peak and off peak time periods. On the other hand, activity based approach views individuals' activity travel patterns are a result of their time use decisions with a continuous time domain. As individuals have 24 hours in a day or multiples of 24 hours for longer periods of time and decide how to use that travel among or allocate that time to activities and travel and with who, subject to their socio-demographic, transportation system and other and scheduling of trips. So, determining the impact of travel demand management policies on time use behavior is an important step to assessing the impact of such policies on individual travel behavior. The final major difference between this two approaches relates to the level of aggregation. In the trip based approach, most aspect of travel, e.g. number of trips etc. are analyzed at an aggregate level.

Consequently, trip based methods accommodate the effect of socio-demographic attributes of households and individuals in a very limited fashion, which limits the activity of the method to evaluate travel impacts of long term socio-demographic characteristics of the individuals who actually make the activity travel choices and the travel service characteristics of the surrounding environment. So, the activity based models are better equipped to forecast the longer term changes in travel demand in response composition and the travel environment of urban areas. Also, using activity based models, the impact of policies can be assessed by predicting individual level behavioral responses instead of employing trip based statistical averages that are aggregated over defined demographic segments.

- ● Can gather past senior age traveller behavior information predict future senior age traveller behavior?

In the past, Germany government had established tourism survey analysis to analyze survey data in order to arrive at reliable conclusions on future trends in travel behavior. To aim to find how demographic change will influence the tourism market and how the industry can adapt to those changes. The travel analysis provided data on tourism consumer behavior, including attitudes, motives and intentions. Since, 1970 year, it is based on a random sample, representative for the population in private households aged 14 years or older. Then, a continuous high scientific standard combined with a national and international users makes the travel analysis a useful tool and reliable source for tourism industry and policy decisions. It aimed to gather statistical data. e.g. on the age structure and on demographic trends, quantitative and qualitative analysis with time series data from the travel analysis. It shows e.g. not only the future volume , quite different from today's seniors, or how who will travel of family holidays will change, e.g. single parents of low, but grandparents of growing significance for tourism.

Demographic change is said to be one of the important drivers for new trends in consumer traveling change behavior in most European countries (e.g. Lind 2001). Because the growing number of senior citizens in the European Union and other industralised countries, such as the USA and Japan, looks to become one of the major marketing challenges for the tourism industry. United Nations statistics predict that the share of people being 60 age or older will grow dramatically in the coming future, and is expected to rise from 10 percent of the world population in 2000 year to more than 20 percent in 2050 year (United Nations Population Division, 2001). From its statistic, some data showed that travel propensity increased throughout life until the age of about 50 years of age and was then kept stable until very late in life 75 age. The most important results is that the travel propensity when getting older is not going down between 65 and 75 age of course, the overall development of this variable is influenced by a lot of other factors which are rsponsible for quite a variation over time. It is now possible to suggest that the general pattern of travel propensity is one of the key indicators for holiday life cycle travel behaviour, includes three stages. The growth stage tends to increase from early aduithood until 45 age old or when reaching some 80%. The next stage is stabilisation from the ages of around 50 age,until 75 age old, starting with a lower increase. Finally, the decrease stage is a slight decrease occurs once people reach the more advanced age of 75 age to 85 age old (Lohmann & Danielsson 2001).

So, it seems Germany government tourism prediction to future travellers' behaviour indicated these findings, such as on how future senior generations will travel, who had used survey data to examine the patterns of travel behaviour of a generation getting older and applied the findings to draw conclusions on the future. Also, it predicted that on the future of family trips, family semgmentation will be the travel behaviour patterns in the future. These findings together with the statistical data on demographic change allowed for a better understanding of the coming tends in family holidays. It's aim developed in consumer behaviour related to demographic change and predicted what will happen future of tourism one had to consider other influences and drivers as well, for example, trends on the supply side. e.g. low cost airlines or in travelling consumption behaviour in general whether how the past may provide a key to predict travel patterns of senior sitizens to the future.

Given the projected growth of the senior citizens market, designing specific marketing strategies to meet the prospective needs of elderly tourists will become increasingly important. It has been an implict assumption that it will be a close relationship between the travel behaviour of today's senior citizens and the those of future ones. The growing number of senior citizens in the world. e.g. China, Hong Kong, Japan, USA etc. countries. Global senior citizen tourism market will be based solely on demographic predictions about the future of the population's age structure. However, many of these seniors won't only live longer but will be fitter and more active until later in life. Many of the will also have plenty in life. Many of them will also have plenty of time and money to spend on travel. So, will these new seniors behave like today's senior citizens? Will they adopt the same travel behaviour as the previous generation or become a new market of oldies for the leisure and tourism indudtry? However, to determine the actual number of senior citizens who will be travelling and to sought to evaluate and specify certain difficult to predict the actual numbers of senior citizen to any country. However, they can be based on the implicit assumption that there is a close relationship between the travel behaviour of past, present and future seniors. But is this a valid assumption? As the reiseanalyse travel analysis survey, which was conducted in Germany every year, offered some interesting data possibiltieis. It was designed to monitor the holiday travel behaviour, opinions and attitudes of Germans and has been carried out since 1970 year, questions in the questionnaire. Data are based on face to face interviews, with a representative sample of more than 7,500 repondents, the interviews being carried out in January each year. All results refer to the average for the defined generated, which ranges generally over ten years. The group of people then at the age of 60 to 69 age is described. This corresponds to the same generation ten years ago, when they had an age of 50 to 59 age. When this methodological approach is not necessarily very sophisticated, it does have the important advantages of being cost effective.

- Can gather traveller past psychological change to predict future travelling behavior?

On the psychological view point, I think individual traveler's character will have those kind of personal characteristics. First, simplicity searchers value above everything ease not transparency in their travel planning and holiday making, and are willing to avoid having to go through extensive research. Second, cultural purists use their travel as an opportunity to immerse themselves in an unfamiliar looking to break themselves entirely from their home lives and engage. Sincerely with a different way of living. Third, social capital seekers understand that to be well travelled is a personal quality, and their choices are shaped by their desire to take maximum of social reward from their travel. They will exploit the potential of digital media to enrich and inform their experiences, and structure their adventures always keeping in mind they are being watched by online audiences. Finally, reward hunters seek a return on the investment who make in their busy , high-achieving lives. Linked in part to the growing trend of wellness, including both physical and mental self improvement who seek truly extraordinary and often indulgent or luxurious' must have experiences.

Why needs to know the personal character of individual traveler's characteristics. Because if travel agents could feel which kinds of individual traveler's character, then who can predict which kind of travel package to design to them more easily. For example, how to determine future travel behaviour from past travel experience and perceptions of risk and safety? We need to concern that the influences of past international travel experience, types of risk associated with international travel and the overall degree of safety feeling during international travel on individual's travelling experiences likelihood of travelling to various geographic regions on their next international vacation trip or avoidance of those regions, due to perceived risk. Because individual traveler's experience of safety risk degree to the countries, it will influence who chooses to go to the countries/country to travel again.

Why travellers avoid certain destinations are as relevant decision making as why who choose to go to the country(countries) to travel. Perceptions of risk and safety and travel experiences are likely to influence travel decisions; efforts to predict future travel behaviour can benefit to individual tourist's decision making. As Weber & Bottorn (1989) defined risky decision is as "choices among alternatives that can be described by prodability distributions over possible outcomes" (p.114). Some psychologists judge subjective perceptions of physical reality, i.e. image of a particular tourist destination, whereas value judgement refers to the way individual rank destinations according to whose attributes. i.e. attractiveness, safety, risk etc. factors to form on overall image. So, if the individual traveler had unhappy and worried and unsafe experiences to go to where the place(country) to travel during whose vacation time before. Then, this negative travel experience will influence who is afraid to go to the place (country) to travel again. Risk of place, country, destination or region means the danger is relatively high to the place, ie. increasing in airplane accidents, crime or terrorist activity targeting citizens of potential traveler's nationality or the probability of occurrence is great , ie. recent occurrences involving travel regions/destinations under consideration or effective actions to control consequences exist. i.e. selecting safe regions and destinations, taking extra precautions when traveling to risky destinations. These risk factors will influence the individual traveler who chooses to cancel travel plan to go to the country again.

Another interesting research, how to predict behavioural intention of choosing a travel destination, which has focus of toursm research for years, but the complex decision making process leading to the choice of a travel destination has not been well researched. The planned behaviour model using its core constructs, attitude, subjective norm and perceived behavioural control, with the addition of the past behavioural variable on behavioural intention of choosing a travel destination.

Understanding why people travel and what factors influence their behavioural intention of choosing a travel destination is beneficial to tourism planning and marketing. Understanding travel motivation is the push and pull model. The idea of the push and pull model is the decomposition of an individual's choice of a travel destination into two forces. The first force is the push factor that pushes an indvidual away home and attempts to develop a general desire to go somewhere else, without specifying where that may be. The second force is the pull factor, that pulls on individual toward a destination, due to a region specific travel location or perceived attractiveness of a destination. The respective push and pull factors illustrate that people travel because who are pushed by their internal motives and pulled by external forces of a destination. Nevertheless, how push and pull factors guide people's attitude and how these attributes lead to behavioural intentions of choosing a travel destination have rarely been investigated. The decision making process leading to the choice of a travel destination is a very complex process. The planned behaviour model is as a research framework to predict the behavioural intention of choosing a travel destination. The model based on the three constructs of attitude, subjective norm, and perceived behavioural control (Fishbein & Ajzen, 1975).

In conclusion, the traveller's past travelling experience can influence travelers who decide to choose to travel the country, which include personal safety was perceived to the highest motivation factors among the important factors which include, scenic beauty, cultural interests, friendliness of local people, price of trip, services in hotels and restaurants, quality and variety of food and shopping facilities and services. The factors include both push and pull. Push factors include knowledge, prestige, and enhancement of human relationship etc., whereas, the most significant pull factors include high technologic image, expenditure and accessibility etc. For example, Japanese travelers visiting Hong Kong. Push factors are such as exploration dream fulfillment and pull factors are such as benefits sought, attractions and good climate city. It will be the factor of future travel patterns and motivations of sub-cultural and ethic groups for Japanese choice to go to Hong Kong travelling.

● Can gather past travelling experience information predict future travelling behavior?

Can travel agencies and airlines organizations attempt to gather data concerns how many visitors number to every country in order to make more accurate evaluation concerns what factors cause why the country will have visitors increasing number or decreasing number till to nowadays from their past travelling behaviors' choices? It is one worthy and considerate question in tourism industry. If the country's airlines and travel agencies can gather every year travellers number data to evaluate what factors influence they choose to their country to travel, e.g. cheap air tickets, attractive seasonal weather environment, cheap and comfortable hotel living feeling etc. many different kinds of entertainment supplying factors to let them to choose to play in their journeys.

If these travelling business organizations can find which one factor is the most important to influence many visitors prefer to choose the country to travel. Then, the country can know whether what any travelling aspect strengths, it needs continue to keep or what any travelling aspect weaknesses, it needs to review in order to achieve the increase of visitors number every continue year in the future. They many follow lot of travellers' past similar or same travelling behavioral characteristics , those data to carrying predicting whether what factors they need to keep or review in order to attract future more visitors prefer to choose to go to itself country to travel successfully. I shall indicate some past travelling data gathering predicting methoss to explain why and how they can help any travelling business organizations to find the what the most important factors to influence whose country's consumer behaviors as below:

Firstly, we need to know what factors can influence local tourists' decision making on choosing a destination? Some visitors choose the country for destination, the reasons may include that the country itself social, cultural as well as the traveller personal and psychological factors , as well as the travel agencies' the number of tourists' destination attractions to the country, available amenities, travelling service package , price and variors types of tourism destinations arrangement etc. examples of the elements which can be considered in decision making.

For example, what is the purpose of tourism of the country? What is /are the factor(s) persuade(s) many travellers perfer to choose to the country in their past travelling experience? So, if the country could attempt to gather its diffent tourism destination data from the past travellers' travelling experiences. Then, it can define future insights to tourists' behavior and analyze what factors will influence tourists' future destination choices in order to increase more attraction to those future possible popular travelling destinations in itself country.

Hence, researching past whether which destinations had been often visited by past travellers' experiences. Then, the country can follow these the country itself past travellers' liking popular travelling destinatons data to make more accurate future popular destinations prediction for its future travellers. Then, the country government can prepare to design the similar past travellers' liking travelling destinations buildings to be build more in itself countries in order to attract future many visitors' visiting needs when they choos to travel itself country. So, research past what buildings design can attract many travellers to like to visit, it can help the country to predict whether what buildings that the future travellers like to visit, or what kinds of hotel design that they choose to live in preferable.

Another consideration is that to understand what features of life course events are important in determining travel behavior changes to consider how the events themselves are influenced by travel preferences , to consider how different events interact to shape travel behavior or to shape view and understand travel behavior development over the life span, e.g. gathering the past travellers' behaviors may include how and why the residential relocation in the country, how any why travel behavior inter-relationship and the role of socialisation in travel behavior.

So, any country may gather its past social development data in order to predict how to motivate future foreign travellers choose to travel itself country more easily. It means that understanding how to develop the country itself social development or social structure in order to let many countries' different visitors feel it can own some social development strengths or characteristics , and they can attract the different countries' foreign travellers feel that they increase more interest to travel itself country in preference as well as it can also attract them to visit itself country to observe whether what the travelling country's actual social development is different to themselves countries. What are the actual social development to this travelling country owns? Instance, the country's social development may include that its social environment developments that prevail, where the travelling choice country's employment locations may be different to the travellers' themselves countries employment locations; what the travelling choice country's residential locations may be different to the travellers' themselves countries residential locations; what the travelling choice country's housing types, car ownership types , mode to work which are different to the travellers themselves countries in society.

In conclusion, if the country could fulfil itself lifestyle choices and short -term travelling activity and travel choices (travelling activity style, activity duration, destination, route , mode) to let many different foreign travellers to feel that the country has much social development or social culture or social structure is different to themselve countries own. Them , it can persuade or attract or increase their travelling desires to attempt to visit this country , due to they hope to find what the this country's actual social development is different to themselves countries' social development nowadays. Hence, if the airlines or travelling agencies organizations can attempt to gather data concerns how its past social and cultural development changed. Then, it may help them to predict that what social development and cultural development and social structure is the most important factor which had been improved to influence many past visitors choose to visit themselves country to travel in the past. Then , they may find what are the most inportant attractive social change factors to influence future visitors' purposes to themselve country in possible.

Bibliography

Backman, K., Backman, S., Uysal, M. And Sunshine, K. (1995). Event Tourism : An Examination Of Motivations And Activities. Festival Management And Event Tourism, 3(1), 15-24.

Fishbein, M., & Ajzen, Z. (1975). Belief, Attitude, Intention And Behaviour: An Introduction To Theory And Research, Boston: Addison Wesley.

Hsu, C.H.C., Cai , L.A., Li, M(2010). Expectation, Motivation And Attitude: A Tourist Behavioral Model. Journal Of Travel Research, 49(3), 282-296. http://dx.doi, org/10.1177/004728750 9349266.

ICT Information And Communication Technology Switzerland, 2005. ICT Fakten (ICT facts). Available from http://www.ictswitzerland.ch/de/ict%2fakten/factsfigures.asp(retrieved Dec.12, 2005) in German.

Lind, (2001): Befolkningen, Familjen, Livscykeln- Och Ekonomisk Tillvaxt. Institutet For Tillvaxtpo-litiska studier/Vinnova/Nutek.

Lohmann, Martin (2001): The 31 st. Reiseanalyse-RA 2001. Tourism: vol. 49, no.1/2001;pp.65-67, Zagreb.

United Nations Population Division (2001). World Population Prospects: The 2000 year Revision, New York.

Weber E.U., & W, P.Bottom (1989). "Axiomatic Measures Of Perceived Risk: Some Tests And extensions." journal of behavioral decision making, 2 (2): 113-31.